The Letter to the Colossians

ADRIENNE VON SPEYR

The Letter to
the Colossians

Translated by
Michael J. Miller

IGNATIUS PRESS   SAN FRANCISCO

Title of the German original:
Der Kolosserbrief
second edition
© 1993 Johannesverlag, Einsiedeln
With ecclesiastical approval

Cover by Roxanne Mei Lum

CONTENTS

THE APOSTLE AND HIS COMMUNITY

1:1–2. *Paul, an apostle of Christ Jesus by the will of God, and Timothy our brother, to the saints and faithful brethren in Christ at Colossæ: Grace to you and peace from God our Father.*[1]

Paul presents himself and Timothy his brother as the joint senders of the letter. He sets limits from the start, though—distances that indicate the varying interrelationships between God and believers: there is the difference between himself and *Timothy* and the one between those two and the *faithful in Colossæ*. *By the will of God* Paul is an apostle and sends the letter with Timothy; that delineates their position. Paul is not to be thought of without this will, which has made him into *an apostle of Christ Jesus*. That is his whole life, the form and content of his existence.

Everything Paul will say will be dependent upon the fact that he is the apostle of the Lord and that he holds this office by the Father's will and at his good pleasure, which also determined the life of the Son.

Timothy our brother is his co-worker and as such shares in the office. He is Paul's brother and stands by his side; then again he is a brother like the brethren in Colossæ and so maintains an intermediate position between the apos-

[1] Scripture quotations have been taken from the Revised Standard Version, Catholic edition.—TRANS.

tle who has been sent and the community that receives. The letter is directed *to the saints and faithful brethren in Christ*. In Christ they are brothers, just as Paul is Christ's apostle. The unity of brotherhood is established in the Lord, just as the union between the community and the apostle is established in the Lord: there is a place, within the Lord, from which both faith and mission pour forth. Apostle and community members are made brethren in the Lord; but this brotherhood is not external, not something that would bind them only on earth; it is something essential, a participation in the life of the Lord, an exercise of obedience to him in intimacy with him, which constitutes the entire life and being of the Christian and of the Church.

This unity is illustrated again by the content of the greeting: *Grace to you and peace from God our Father.* It is a wish—and at the same time a corroboration. This *grace* and this *peace* live in God; there they are unceasingly real. The Son continually proclaimed both. The apostle, who lives by the truth of God, can not merely beseech the Lord to send them down; he can demand them: from God, who has sent him and provided him with what is necessary, so that the community also can live according to the mind of the Lord. He can demand them, though, from the brethren also, who have to respond to God with their faith, that is, with their lives, in which they must give witness to the gift they have received from the Father through the Son. And this unity, which binds Paul and the brethren together in the Lord and makes them one, should be visible not only in their daily lives through the grace of the Father. This unity is constantly shown to them from heaven, through faith, in the life of the triune God by the Spirit, who sends the gifts of grace and peace, by the Son, who lived on earth and manifested them, and by the Father, who thereby reveals his will, so that believers may know what their lives are to be based on and what they may hope for. Paul's greeting is so formulated as to renew and enliven this knowledge and to increase in them effectively the grace and peace of God. The wish is also a blessing, something reminiscent of a sacrament: what is perfectly real in heaven becomes, through the apostle's gesture, more fully realized on earth than before. From the greeting a power goes out, which strengthens the relation of the apostle to the brethren and corroborates it.

1:3. *We always thank God, the Father of our Lord Jesus Christ, when we pray for you.*

The unity among Father, Son and community is shown once again in the prayer of the apostles. They *thank God, the Father*, and this thanksgiving is a prayer to God, which, however, from the outset includes the Colossians. It is evident from this that Paul's prayer never stops at an object or at one fixed idea, but rather is something comprehensive and dynamic, thanks and petition, worship and instruction, like the course of a river that begins in faith and ends in God. Moreover it is always a trinitarian prayer, addressed to God, in his capacity as Father of the Son, in the Spirit; where it turns to one of the Divine Persons, all three are intended thereby. A prayer meant for the Son can be accepted by the Father, while the Spirit communicates it. Or Paul may on a certain occasion utter a prayer of thanksgiving and without further ado expect God to receive it as an act of pure worship. He can commend to him the community and its particular petitions, knowing all the while that God retains the power to dispose freely of any matter presented in prayer. This prayer is characterized by such faith in and understanding of God that faith makes the prayer the act of its submission and gives itself so unconditionally therein that God can form out of this surrender vocations as well as conversions, or anything at all he wishes. From Paul's attitude of prayer flows the formation of his life, and the same should be true for every Christian who prays. Prayer is movement: starting from a seemingly arbitrary point on earth (it can be any one at all) onward to the triune God. It is a grace, but also a deed, and it therefore possesses the visibility that characterizes a deed; it is the earth's question to heaven, to which the answer comes down from heaven to earth. True prayer always works signs and wonders, for the one who prays experiences the grace of God in the fact that the Holy Trinity graciously accepts the prayer and applies it in the world when required. And if the apostle at the beginning of the letter assures the brethren of his prayers, he is showing to them in advance—even before he admonishes and instructs them and allows them to share his insight—that they possess, through his prayers as well as through those of his brother Timothy and through each and every prayer, their own included, a place in heaven, a home with God.

1:4. Because we have heard of your faith in Christ Jesus and of the love which you have for all the saints.

Paul has learned that they believe in the Lord and love the saints; which is again a movement, a fruitfulness, a reciprocity between contemplation and action. A movement, in that the *faith in Christ Jesus* extends to their relations with their neighbors and transforms them. A fruitfulness, since faith gives birth to charity, which then determines their entire outlook. And a reciprocity, since the contemplative side, faith and prayer, requires deeds and charity, according to the Lord's commandment of love, for he wants a praying, loving, living community. And if the Colossians love the saints, that is, the believers, and prove to be charitable and helpful toward them, they thereby increase their faith in turn, *their* power of prayer and contemplation, so that those loved may also learn to pray better and become capable of loving more. Paul takes part in the prayer of the brethren by praying to the Father; their faith in the Son strengthens Paul's relation to the Father. And their love for the brethren makes the Apostle view the Colossians more vividly as his brethren. Thus everything presses constantly onward toward the same unity, and the closeness and fullness of this unity, the clinging to it, proves to be yet a new source from which everything pours out again, allowing new fruitfulness to stream forth from within.

1:5. *Because of the hope laid up for you in heaven. Of this you have heard before in the word of the truth, the gospel.*

The hope laid up in heaven is intimately connected with faith, which binds mankind to heaven, but also with charity, since hope nourishes charity. Christians possess faith, love and hope so as to be bonded to heaven always by all three, in such a manner that their activity and their outlook and their prayer on earth are definitively stamped by them. All of this, though, has its source in *the word of truth*—that is, the message of the Son, who said of himself that he is the *Truth* and that he is the *Word*—*the gospel*, since this constitutes the meaning and the substance of the good news. It is a substance that cannot be heard without being verified. It is a word of such power that in becoming flesh it brings to earth not only a thought, a form of knowledge, but nothing less than a life, one that strives toward God and submits itself to him and tries to do his will, through which Paul became an apostle. And thus everything meshes again: the three virtues into their unity. They work together in the community and give witness to their common source, but their effectiveness derives from the revelation of the Son, which is communicated through Paul and his proclamation. It is a dynamic unity: in prayer, in love of neighbor, in deed and word and good news. In this summary the character of the word of God becomes clear: it becomes evident that the believer is endowed with a field of action as wide as the word; on the other hand, that everything happens within the triune substance of God and can be traced back to it, since the love of the Son expresses itself in obedience to the Father, and the freedom of the Spirit manifests itself in the fact that he allows himself to be sent. To live in the word of God means the austerity of personal prayer devoted to worship and intercession— and then, too, it means an apostolate and missionary task of worldwide scope, so that responsibility for others and responsibility before God merge into one another. This *word of the truth, the gospel*, embraces God's Word in his totality: his life on earth in the flesh, but also his entire teaching, immediate knowledge of the triune God in eternity and a share in the fullness of divine life.

1:6. *Which has come to you, as indeed in the whole world it is bearing fruit and growing—so among yourselves, from the day you heard and understood the grace of God in truth.*

The gospel is both in Colossæ and *in the whole world*, and this characteristic—being at the same time in a particular place and everywhere—belongs to its dynamism, which we have mentioned. The gospel has the power of being simultaneously localized and omnipresent. The fact that it is somewhere else in no way diminishes its presence here. This is no game of hide-and-seek; it is the expression of its surpassing greatness; it brings the place, the realm in which it has being, closer to those who are in another place. In its distinctive particularity, the gospel is capable of making contact, of transforming places, of bringing them closer together and making them more alike. For someone living in Colossæ and possessing the gospel there, the rest of the world gains new meaning and new immediacy through the gospel. The unknown world, which before had been a matter of indifference, draws near, and as a result the faith of the particular locality in turn undergoes an expansion. It is a reciprocal process, in which new aspects of God's truth become evident, aspects that were always there but that now, through the convergence and extension of places, make themselves known to the believers and cause their love to grow.

The gospel has other attributes that similarly intersect one another: it *bears fruit*, and it *grows*. It is, consequently, fruitful even before it has grown to full maturity, but the fullness of its growth will never be completely comprehensible to mere men, because nobody will ever attain in faith to a full understanding of its contents or be able to keep pace with its depths, its dimensions, its fullness of *truth*. So the gospel cannot wait until it is fully comprehended by mankind in order to bear fruit. It bears fruit at the same time that it grows, as though it were something incidental, or a contributing factor, or even as though the fruits were precisely what made the growth possible. If comprehension is fruitful, then the fruits also contribute to the increase of this comprehension.

So among yourselves. The Colossians know that it is so among themselves also, and the Apostle assures them of it. It has been so *from the day you heard*; the act of hearing, though, contained within it *the grace of God*, understood *in truth*. Accordingly there is no dividing the doctrine from the Author, the word from the Lord, the comprehension from grace, or human truth from the divine. God's grace is not something hanging in the air; it is bound up precisely with the comprehension of the good news, it is administered through the Lord, who is the Word and who cultivates the word, yet grace always complies with divine truth. Grace is to be comprehended in accordance with this divine truth. If the Colossians had ever thought that their faith was a local affair, that they in Colossæ had received it and it was something that concerned only them and their God, then they would have to realize now the extent to which it belongs to a greater construction, forms part of a complete building, and realize how God's gracious intention has prepared created things for faith, so that the entire man, the entire locale and the entirety of life are engaged; that there can certainly be one *day* (as is here the case) from which faith can be dated, because that was the day it was first heard, but that that day included everything that is meant by grace and truth and place and human existence. One cannot grasp any corner without drawing the entire cloth after it. And it is important for the Colossians to become acquainted with this side of the truth of faith; they will then feel in their entire life of faith that they are that much more included, and at the same time they will know how much more the other communities are included and so will begin to comprehend what fellowship in God is.

1:7. *As you learned it from Epaphras our beloved fellow servant. He is a faithful minister of Christ on our behalf.*

Through a believer they have experienced the grace of God's truth. Paul calls *Epaphras* his *fellow servant*; he works for the Lord and for his teaching as does Paul. The directions and instructions he gives are identical to those of Paul; there is no difference between the actions of the servant and those of the fellow servant. Epaphras is *a faith-ful minister of Christ*, one who is sent and does his duty. Paul knows therefore that the doctrine that was imparted to the Colossians is the right one, that they are in union with him, that the fellow servant through his work has extended the province of truth on earth. Paul does not think he has to do the entire job by himself; he is not worried that the doctrine might be preached differently by others; he trusts God's grace, which can be communicated in many ways in the one truth. Unity of doctrine is maintained in God's sight in the mediation of his grace to the world. The one who scatters the seed of doctrine gathers in at the same time, for what is scattered draws the hearers back into the unity of the word and belongs to that unity, possessing, not merely some vague share in it, but a sure, valid and bonded share that for Paul as for Epaphras and for each of the Colossians and for any Christian on earth at all contains the total unity of the truth. And if Paul here expressly mentions the preaching of Epaphras and shows the Colossians that he is acquainted with them and has followed their progress to faith, he does so to allow them to cooperate in his own mission and labors. They are not some stray fragment of a church with a doctrine that is valid merely for them; they are in complete unity with him, and this unity is the one that is valid with God, that is accomplished in him with the Son and the Spirit.

1:8. *And has made known to us your love in the Spirit.*

Epaphras has rendered an account. That is only fitting in the building up of the Church. The Colossians must be glad that he did so; they should gain thereby a deeper understanding for the growing Church, which is already bearing fruit. On this occasion they happen to learn that Epaphras has told about the love that inspires them. It is *love in the Spirit*, that is to say, originating in him and so, like all matters of faith, having its foundation and its home in heaven. This love is not their achievement; it is a grace. That does not make it a love that is floating around somewhere, detached from its origin; it has its place in the Spirit, who brings it about and simultaneously accepts its fruit. The latter testifies to the mutuality of faith in the Lord: nothing is lost that is done by the Spirit. So far the letter has been mainly about the Father and about the Son's doctrine; now, though, this teaching is given out and gathered in again through the Spirit, who in his movement back to heaven takes home with him as fruit all that he has sown, and who furthermore brings about the exchange that believers will experience as participation in the life of the Divine Persons. This love in the Spirit, which they put into action and which in a deeper sense is active in them, contributes to the increase of their living knowledge of God in faith. Charity is the decisive proof that faith bears fruit on earth.

1:9. *And so, from the day we heard of it, we have not ceased to pray for you, asking that you may be filled with the knowledge of his will in all spiritual wisdom and understanding.*

The report that Paul had received about the conversion of the Colossians was a decisive moment in his life as an apostle; for on their account he must take upon himself from now on a new responsibility before God. A prayer commitment. Whenever he spoke previously of the presence of God's word in the whole world, this world was viewed in his prayer as a universal field for the gospel. He has to keep it before his eyes. His prayer, too, must always be open to the world in its totality, so that the fruitfulness of the gospel may show forth in it. If a certain part of the world, though, is won over, then the universal prayer for the world turns here into a particular prayer. The praying Christian has a certain responsibility for those parts of the world that have not yet accepted the good news; he has another for those who are converting or have converted. And Paul has *not ceased to pray.* It is part of his job. Now he is obliged to include the Colossians expressly in his constant prayer. This has a double effect. They receive a share in the fruits of all his prayers; they have a kind of presence everywhere he prays. But they also form the object of his prayer; in this universal prayer in which they share, there is a particular prayer for them, in which Paul pleads for what they need most: that they *may be filled with the knowledge of his will,* so that this will may become the substance of their being and so that they, like the Son, will have no nook or cranny within them that is not filled by this will. The whole man, the whole community, should surrender itself in an all-encompassing faith. Through the will of God, then, they attain to *all spiritual wisdom and understanding*. God the Father grants them to know his will, and God the Spirit gives the insight needed to carry it out. Thus filled, they no longer have any room left within themselves that is not occupied by this will; but they have all the room they need for the breathing of the Spirit, for *wisdom*. Divine will and divine insight mesh and thereby portray the workings of the triune life in heaven; God's gifts can never really be grasped in any other way than in such a harmonious interaction, a mutual operation and cooperation. And the believers of Colossæ have become the bearers of this divine interplay, images in which the divine nature is reflected, fields wherein God's seed is effectively sprouting.

1:10. *To lead a life worthy of the Lord, fully pleasing to him, bearing fruit in every good work and increasing in the knowledge of God.*

Now men have to take on those characteristics that Paul affirmed earlier of the gospel: *bearing fruit* and *increasing*. In faith they have become bearers of this good news, as the Son was; in such a way, however, that, in bearing, they are transformed and themselves acquire the characteristics of the gospel. Indeed, so that they reflect perfectly in their comportment that which brings this comportment about; so that they are consequently recognized from afar as believers. For not they, but the faith should be proclaimed and should live. And in this way they will *lead a life worthy of the Lord*, as his followers. Their worth will be to bear what he brought, what he himself bore, what marked and identified him as the Word of the Father. They are *worthy*, while keeping a certain distance and not for one moment mistaking themselves for Christ and the gospel, and still they possess such a *knowledge of God* that it transforms them continuously and makes them *fully pleasing to him*. As long as the Son walked the earth, the Father saw in him the perfect expression of his will and of his knowledge, and so his favor rested on him. And now the Son, who redeemed the world, should in turn see true followers in his faithful; he should be able to observe on earth his own life living on anew and see the reason for his Incarnation realized in them, the name that he planted springing up in them. The Son, who does the will of his Father on earth, knows the Father. From all eternity he lived in his bosom. Believers, though, know the Son, and through the Son they know the Father, because the Son has implanted in them his living substance—which substance is at the same time Christian doctrine. He lived right under their eyes, kept no secrets from them, granted them insight into everything, even into his prayer. They still know what they should imitate from his example, what he now demands; they also know how he spoke on earth, drew strength and light from the Father, proved his submission to the Father. Similarly they can prove their submission to him, walk in his footsteps; and these are not fading impressions but rather, by dint of the gospel, a trail that is fresh and clear, so that the imitation of Christ, like the gospel itself, promotes fruitfulness and growth among them. What they bear are the fruits of the gospel. And if the Lord said, "By their fruits you shall know them", then they must recognize now, in their own fruits, those of the gospel.

1:11a. *May you be strengthened with all power, according to his glorious might, for all endurance and patience.*

It is the interplay of the natural and the supernatural, creation and redemption, with the predominance of the second over the first, of the New Covenant over the Old. Believers are to be strengthened, but according to God's *glorious might.* This might should give an eternal quality to their own powers, strengthening them for *all*—not just some—*endurance and patience.* They need that, so as never to fall away from the centrality of their faith and in order to persevere patiently: despite persecutions, the misunderstanding of others, but also despite their own human limitations that confront them, which are indeed being overcome by God's might and yet remain visible as long as they live on earth. Because they, with the Son, do the will of the Father, they are no longer imprisoned within their personal limitations, within the boundaries that man still experienced under the Old Covenant, but rather are transported by something new, something wider and fuller, into a world that belongs to the Lord, the world that he brought to earth. This is the fruitfulness of the gospel within and among them. It comes about in a twofold manner: externally, as the believer awakens faith in others; internally, as he becomes more pliable and submissive to the might of God's glory, "in endurance and patience".

1:11b–12. With joy, giving thanks to the Father, who has qual-
ified us to share in the inheritance of the saints in light.

Thanksgiving follows because God has granted these
gifts, but also because Paul prompts his readers. The gift
is a participation *in light*. This is not played out in some
sphere inaccessible to men, but corresponds to an ability
for which God has *qualified* us, so that it becomes visible.
Light is the most objective thing there is. It is the eternal
light, which is eternally in the presence of the Father. But
now it is no longer separated from the world; the Son has
brought it with him and, in ascending into heaven, has
left it behind on earth. And faith brings about the ability
to have a share in it. For this reason the Colossians should
be grateful *with joy*, with objective joy giving objective
thanks for the objective light. And all of this objectivity
is the fruit of faith, specifically in the new doctrine, and is
accordingly the immediate consequence of the Son's sacrifice. The Son has the sacrifice, and the believers have the
joy. Yet sacrifice and joy meet in thanksgiving, in the Father, in the intensifying knowledge about the Father, Son
and Spirit. That role in the act of thanksgiving, however,
that falls to the lot of Paul; namely, his admonition to give
thanks, belongs to the work of the Church, whereby the
personality of the individual is submerged so as to make
room for the structure that the Son has set up on earth.
And not only the believer but the Church, too, has a share
in the light, in a way that is clear both to her and to the
individual and that fills both with joy. Thus it is not a
coerced, dutiful thanksgiving, but one offered out of joy,
in which it is evident that the gift is recognized, received

and joyfully possessed, with a joy that ultimately is the joy of the Son in the creation of the Father. The light is a *share in the inheritance of the saints*; it is their property, their treasure in faith. A good that God owns and gives away, and on earth there is no limit placed on sharing in it. As the Father possesses the inheritance, so also do the saints. As prodigally as the Father lavishes it, so it is received. It is the treasure that God has destined from eternity for the saints and that now through the coming of the Son has been released, so that it may in reality be utilized and enjoyed by the saints.

1:13. *He has delivered us from the dominion of darkness and transferred us to the kingdom of his beloved Son.*

Again movement: we were wrested from *darkness*—no dimming of light, this, but a *dominion* of darkness that could hold us in custody and was very jealous of its possessions—and *transferred* by the Father himself, who snatched us away and transplanted us in *the kingdom of his beloved Son*, so that we already dwell in this kingdom. The Son, now, is the Child of the Father's love, watched over and cared for by that love, living in it and by it. And we are taken into this kingdom of love. One could have thought of all sorts of partial solutions: dusk, half-light; perhaps with the emphasis on an increase in light and a decrease in darkness; or even increasing darkness, with decreasing light. But Paul speaks only of extremes: the power of darkness, the love of the Son. Living in darkness, we had adapted to it: our senses were narrowly restricted, our will had grown shortsighted. And now we are not

only to see the perfect light but also to live in him, so
that the image of the growing and fruit-bearing gospel is
a suitable one for us as well and is to be proved true again
by our life in the light. All conditions essential for life
have been turned around. The kingdom of light is the
kingdom of the Son; from all eternity it was his kingdom
in heaven, the "air" in which he lives as God, which the
Father grants to him with his love, in which the Spirit
of them both wafts. It is the kingdom where God for
God *is* God. And now the Father takes us to his Son; he
makes himself the way, in much the same manner as the
Son has made himself the Way for us to the Father, he
places himself effectively in the middle so as to reach his
goal. As the Son proved to the Father that his creation is
good, so now the Father proves to the Son how much he
loves his redeemed humanity: so much that he can find
no other place for it now but the place of the Son. The
entire created world is elevated into the Son's world of
light. Creatures are now redeemed beings. And together
with the Son, in his kingdom and his light, the inheritance of the saints is enjoyed.

THE PRIMACY OF CHRIST

1:14. *In [him] we have redemption, the forgiveness of sins.*

Those are two things the world lacks; indeed it needs each one in the other. Two things that are, to be sure, different and yet, again, undivided, in fact indistinguishable, if the value of each is to be complete. The value of redemption lies in the remission of sins; and the remission of sins has taken place, because it signifies redemption. Both, though, are summed up and yet unfolded in the unity of the Lord: summed up, in that his whole life says this one thing: that he came in order to redeem the world, to reconcile it on the Cross with God and then as the fruit of the Cross to grant to his own the remission of sins and the way to attain it. But this unity *in him* is presented again and again in his teaching, unfolded, so that believers may realize the meaning of Christ's life. He came in order to give his Father's world back to him, and this was his intention from time immemorial. He decided it together with the Father and carried it out in obedience to the Father's will. And the Incarnation, the death on the Cross and the Resurrection are the human stages of the keeping of his resolution. But he did not want to do his work without the participation of believers; he leveled the way for them in confession, in the voluntary admission of sins. They are not seized by re-

demption against their will; the Lord clears the path for
them and wants to catch them when they are under way.
But the way itself lies *in him*; it would not be fitting to
experience a remission of sins or a redemption outside
of him; and this *in him* is as essential, as personal and as
corporeal as one can possibly understand it to be. The
debt of guilt is not merely written off but is actually taken
away; this is not a redemption that is only the content
of an article of faith or of a celestial agreement between
Father and Son, but one that the Son lives through and
accomplishes. The corporeality of the Cross, the whole
loving life of the Son of Man, requires a corporeal sharing of believers therein. When Paul says *in him*, he means
it in the strictest sense of the word. It is unfitting for a
Christian to figure out for himself a philosophy of faith
that continually dilutes and spiritualizes this truth, until
he feels exempt from the duty of finding his salvation
in the body of the Son himself, in his blood shed on the
Cross, in his entire humanity, which identifies him as one
of us and at the same time as the One who does the will
of the Father. The entire way that the Redeemer walks as
a man is important, and one must not try to evaluate the
results without taking the presuppositions into account
also: no redemption on the Cross without the life as a
man that preceded it, no life as a man without the origin
of the Son in the triune God.

1:15. *He is the image of the invisible God, the first-born of all creation.*

Invisible is the eternal *God* in the everlasting heavens, whose existence becomes clear to us through faith, who nevertheless remains invisible to us according to his essence. "No one has seen the Father except the Son." We, however, stand in his sight, for he sees our every move and knows our heart, not only as of today, in the place where we are, but from of old, before we existed; and he also continues to know us after our existence is completed, so that we are surrounded on all sides by his invisibility. To keep us from imagining ourselves lost, God grants us faith, so that in faith his divine invisibility becomes for us an essential experience. This invisible God is the content of our faith as Creator of the whole world and Keeper of our whole life, to whom we must render an account, not as though to a stranger or to a passing acquaintance, but rather as to Someone who through faith is well known to us. Therefore we do not have to construct him for ourselves or invent him according to the measure of human imagination; what we need in order to encounter him is provided for us by faith.

But God has done more. He promised his Son; he made known already to the prophets the way his Son would take in becoming man; he announced through the voices of the Old Testament the manifestation of the Son in such a way that we were prepared for his coming and were able to recognize in him then the *image* of the Father. And to recognize it also in everything he brought: in his teaching, which was the teaching of the Father [cf. Jn 7:16], in the Word that he is and that pronounces the word of the Father, in the will that he proclaims and that expresses the will of the Father, in the form that he took on and that is the image of the invisible Father, since he, having become man, appears to our eyes like one who has been created, that is to say, since he acts according to the image of the Father. But his incarnate image is not one that we could finally grasp, define and copy in order to see the Father; "whoever sees me sees the Father" is true only because he is infinitely more than what is made visible in him. In all his words and miracles and deeds lies a surpassing greatness, which suddenly reflects the surpassing greatness of the invisible Father. The eminence that he allows us to glimpse when he turns to us is the eminence that makes him the true image of the Father when he turns to him.

He is, however, the image of the invisible God as *the first-born of all creatures*. The firstborn of the Father, and thus his perfect image, from all eternity the primordial sign of his paternal being. Of the Father's being as God-the-Father. The relation of God the Father to God the Son implies from the beginning that the Son is the firstborn, the Father's exact image who, through what he is, holds within himself all that the Father is. Thus he is able, while being the exact image of the Father on earth, to signify the invisible God in his own visibility; and in everything that we comprehend of him, in all the faith, love and hope that we have in him, we are permitted to love the Father, to hope in the Father, to believe the Father.

And now creation in its entirety receives in its visibility something communicated by the image of the invis-

ible God, who is represented by the Son. Through his
Incarnation it gains an unforeseen depth; what is created
receives a new life, whose inmost meaning lies in the
place where the Son is the firstborn. We, being born afterward, receive through his being the firstborn a new
fullness, which begins to dawn on us only when he, the
summary of all the promises found in creation and in the
Old Testament, brings their fulfillment with him into
the world.

1:16. *For in him all things were created, in heaven and on earth,
visible and invisible, whether thrones or dominions or principalities or authorities—all things were created through him and for
him.*

The picture of creation that predominates in the Old Testament shows the Father, who steps out of his unique-
ness, out of his eternal solitude, and makes a beginning
of his external activity. The beginning of redemption is
completely different. The Son becomes a human being in
his mother's womb just like every other child, and when
she has given birth to him he is helpless and vulnerable
and begins a hard life in poverty, even in flight. There is
no greater difference imaginable than that between these
two beginnings. And if we follow the way of the Son
to the Cross and see how he is despised by the whole
world, loaded down with the guilt of all sins, and dies
with a loud cry, forsaken by God, then his life on earth
seems to stand under this sign: irremediably doomed, pre-
cipitously declining, ending in uselessness and abandonment. Mankind has turned away from him; nothing is

heard from the Father. And yet it is he who saves the world and has lived out Christian doctrine and is the Son of the Father, and Paul's words throw light on his entire existence back to his eternal preexistence. *In him all things were created.* From the beginning, therefore, he has a share not only in the Father's being but also in his creating. The Father creates it for him. And so the word "creation" no longer denotes an unfathomable act of sheer freedom but expresses simultaneously an intention, a relationship of love, so much so that love becomes the reason for creation. And the poverty and sufferings of the Son are likewise related to this love, which was from the beginning, and they are shown to be testimonies of this love: of the Father to the Son, but also of the Father to his creation, of the Son to the Father's creation and to the Father himself, testimony of a love within the Deity that in circulating has drawn into itself that creation which was created because the Son *is*. Paul here has the world participate in a reality that in its perfection leaves far behind the limited paradisiacal creation of the beginning, not only because the world now becomes the expression of eternal love, but also because this testimony is absolutely all-encompassing: things *visible and invisible*, for the latter also have a share in the same being, are the expression of the same love that rules throughout *heaven* and *earth*. This love can rule both, because the Son is at once visible and invisible; visible when he speaks as a man sent by the Father, tells his parables, converses with his apostles and with the beloved disciple and sits with them at table. Invisible on the Cross. In his invisibility, but also in what is visible, are contained many more things than we can ever think of, but they are all concerned with love, because they were created in and through the Son. Not only things are created, but relations, too: *thrones, dominions, principalities, authorities*, everything that is and has an effect; everything that we are in some way or another capable of, but also things that are inaccessible to us, for which we have no sense, which have reality for us only in faith, whether conscious or not: all of that is in the Son, belongs to him, but always inasmuch as he is the Son of the Father.

All things were created through him and for him, says Paul, and with that he crowns his declaration and causes the faith experience of the Colossians to be broadened tremendously. The world is not only created in and through the Son but *for him*. Everything, even what seems to be lost, deteriorated or ruined, belongs also to the revelation and manifestation of the Son and acquires its purpose in reference to him. Is devoted to him. Even before we know it. And so we do not need to go around worried any more, complaining that existence is purposeless, or lose heart because we cannot comprehend the meaning of things; we can take this for granted about every thing and about every relation: it was created for the Son and so possesses in him its truth. We can calm ourselves and let things be as they are, for they belong to the divine love, which provides for the Son in advance and associates all things with him and makes everything ready for him. In this caring love the things themselves also attain their destined purpose, which can only be a purpose of love: every promise implicit in them comes to fulfillment in the Son, and the manifestation of the Son should become such a comprehensive, overwhelming revelation that heaven and earth will be filled with it, in order that the Father may recognize in heaven and earth that which is the Son's, and the Son may comprehend the Father's creation to be nothing other than that which was created for him and which therefore together with him, who is the Way to the Father, is under way to the Father.

1:17. *He is before all things, and in him all things hold together.*

The Son already exists before the creation. Nothing is created without this precedence, which simultaneously clarifies the relation of the Son to creation. Creation is placed after him; by its very essence it has this relation to him, which has its origin in the Father's decree. The Father creates the world after the primordial image of the Son; that being not enough, however, he creates the world in the Son as well, by locating its continuance in him. There is nothing that could fulfill its purpose or possess worth except in the Son, nothing therefore that does not receive from the Son himself its continuance in existence. And if this is true for *all things*, insofar as the universe consists of existing beings, then it is also true for each one of their thoughts, for everything men know or believe, for every endeavor in which they make spiritual and intellectual progress, for all the stages of their development, every extension of their experience: they cannot develop "away from" the Son, since everything *holds together in him*, including each ever-so-precisely formulated and self-contained thought and likewise each consequence thereof and, just so, everything conceivable. So that suddenly the entire breadth of the Son stands before us as the Immeasurable: the Immensity, unto which God created his world. Say rather: modeled his world after him, since the Son's breadth, his divine essence is *before all things*, taking up and sustaining everything. And the fruitfulness that is enfolded in the world is that of continuance in the Son. Not only human thought—faith too, which is a gift from God, and grace and the sacraments and every encounter between God and man: all have their continued existence in the Son. Thus we can see in the Incarnation, as it were, a foreshadowing of the Eucharist: the Son's life can be in us because our life has the privilege of being in him. God has introduced the world into the circulation of his eternal love, but he has taken it up in such a way that he has brought what is characteristic of a human being—being a soul in a body—to its perfect fulfillment in the Incarnation of the Son, for the Son has given to bodily life its complete, supernatural, divine meaning, and on his own body through the Eucharist he has bestowed continued, perduring existence, whereby he also grants to our body and to our whole humanity continuance in his body. It is therefore no longer the case that the things of this world can be valued in a stepwise progression from the corporeal to the spiritual; common to all of them is that they are directed to the Son and have in him their continued being.

1:18. *He is the head of the body, the church; he is the begin-ning, the first-born from the dead, that in everything he might be pre-eminent.*

As Head of the Church, he enters into the closest of relationships with his own creation, with that which he founded on earth. His capacity of being the Head is not ac-quired subsequently; he has it from the beginning, while hidden within the Father, then on earth and again after he returns to heaven. The Head who governs everything, possesses everything, and renders an account for every-thing. Governs, so that the Mystical Body, the Church may be, not forlorn, but orderly. Possesses, so that the Church may have a place, a home in him. Renders an account to the Father of his work on earth, the crown-ing achievement of which is the Church. Because he has taken on flesh, corporeality is so valuable to him, he is so committed to it, it binds him so closely to the Father that he gives this *body* to the *Church*. The Church is not an idea; she is perfectly concrete, because the Church that administers the body of the Lord becomes the body of the Lord and because, moreover, she has the Lord him-self as her Head. Whatever is powerful about the Church, whatever is unique about her, her unity in God is com-prehensible from the fact that she is a body ordered to the Head; just as every body belongs to its head and is di-rected to it. This power extends beyond time; moreover it goes back to that time when the Son was known to the world merely in promise. He was already the Head then. This demonstrates that the Church needed the Old Covenant in order to exist, in order to be founded at all, just as the word of fulfillment presupposes the word of promise. This is not only a sign of how necessary, unique and true the Church is but is, together with that, a sign of the omniscience of the triune God, who has always cared for the salvation of his world.

As a body, the Church appears in her true nature: as something that is in the Lord and has its continuance in him, just as the Son is in the Father. She is a component part of the Lord, which he himself brings forth and maintains, in order to present it at every moment to the Father. So of course it is possible for the Church to be a spotless bride, precisely because she is in him, the body of the Divine Head. Yet Paul does not dwell on the Church for long; he mentions the subject only to demonstrate the primacy of the Son in her as well. *He, who is the beginning* is now the only important thing. He is *the beginning* absolutely, as if he had no relation at all to the world, to anything created or merely possible; and then suddenly he is the beginning again as *the first-born from the dead*. Next to the great, self-contained terminology that Paul has been applying there now steps up the long procession of individuals who have died, who at first have no connection between them except for their being dead, but then in fact are united into a single reality by the Firstborn, the Lord. He is for every dead person, in every age, the One who is already dead; each of them possesses the reality of his death in him. For the Son has not merely carried each sinner's sins, in order to redeem him; he also died each one's death, so that all the dead might share in his being. So that his Incarnation and his death on the Cross might come alive for them, too, and might create for them the primary vital relationship; so that his being dead for every dead person might lead each one back to the Father, because he, united with the Father by a relation that is not interrupted while he is dead, establishes that same relation in their name also and for their benefit. We could understand, of course, that he was *the beginning* absolutely: in heaven where he was eternally in the presence of the Father, in the universe of living creatures that was entirely directed unto him—but there remained the realm of the great void: the dead! And now this void, too, is filled, because he is their firstborn, because he did not forget them but granted them a new beginning in him, without forfeiting thereby his capacity as Head, so that all the dead acquire a relation to this body; in this case, not in that he grants them his body sacramentally in the Eucharist, but in that he takes them into his body, the Church, makes them members of his body and is placed over them as Head. He is the firstborn of the dead in order to become their Head. Thus the entire way he walked as the Son of Man stands in full array before us, effective even unto death and well beyond death, so as to bring the dead also, and them particularly, back home into genuine life. His body, therefore, from the moment the Spirit descends upon the Mother until his descent among the dead on Holy Saturday, is burdened with the task of redeeming the world. He redeems not only when he becomes incarnate or preaches or dies on the Cross; he redeems there, too, where he is a dead man among the dead. The Father's intention at creation, not merely to make man but to give him the power to achieve things by his activity, is fulfilled in the Son beyond all expectation: he is effective even as a dead man! And he crowns this work by conquering the death of each individual sinner individually for him in his body. The wages of sin is death, but for the Son death becomes again an instrument of life: he does not conquer man as man was created by the Father but rather the sinner who has died, so that life may be wrought in him.

That in everything he might be pre-eminent. That is the will of the Father. He has set him in this place and wills that he stay there. And the Son, who in all things strives to do the will of the Father, keeps at it in this as well. He may not move from his place to leave it to someone else, any more than he as the Son of Man may forget that he is God. Heeding the will of the Father, he must be the First. And if he brings us divine doctrine in person and is for us the Word of the Father, if we are to understand him as the Way and the Truth that lead to the Father, then he must also make room for us in himself, so as to walk this Way in the Truth. He must make himself to be this room and, accordingly, must be the all-encompassing First, as the Father has determined he should be. It is therefore impossible for any man to contest his right to his place. He remains the Beginning and the Head of mankind; every hierarchy takes its origin from his primacy, without ever being able to attain a rank equal to the Son's mission. If the Son is the First by obedience, then our obedience will be arranged as part of his. For it belongs to faith not merely to strive for as deep a knowledge as possible of the things of God but also and always to comply with what is learned, in such a manner that the first and fundamental truth will not be impugned. The relationship between

Father, Son and Spirit, which is visible in the Son and his Church, forms the unshakable foundation of our faith. We ought to form this Church of his redeemed ones and stand at the place to which he assigns us, in the obedience that is due to the Head from the member. That is an essential component of the Christian tradition, and it follows that the Church can never move away from the Head, can never become something other than the body of this Head.

1:19. *For in him all the fulness of God was pleased to dwell.*

The Lord not only *is* fullness; fullness resides in him. This distinction has its basis in the distinction of the three Persons in the essential unity of God. The Son is from all eternity and shares in all that is the Father's, all that is the Spirit's, and yet remains the Son. And the fullness that resides in him is the fullness of the Father and of the Spirit and his own fullness. This is to be understood as a fullness of every kind: it is every good, every breadth, everything eternal. It is extended in every duration and into every place and embraces everything divine. It cannot be encompassed in words, because it is infinite, and yet it finds, despite its boundlessness, a dwelling in him, the divine Son, so that he has it at his disposal. This disposition is a mystery; he possesses it in order to lavish it on others but also in order to be the Head of the Church, the Father's Son who was made man, the Brother of everyone who believes. It is a fullness that is different from everything that is limited, small, petty or provisional. And since the fullness resides in him, the fullness is not simply what he is but rather what he has; he is not tied down to it, but through it he is free; and by the fact that he has it, he can show the world how rich God is in his triune life and how much the Father and the Spirit desire to communicate themselves through him to the world. This fullness is so limitless that no thought can be thought, no feeling can be felt, no love can be loved, without being contained in it. If things from the beginning were created as destined to the Son, it is because they find their fulfillment in his fullness. This fullness is twofold: with respect to the world, it is the fulfillment of the promise inherent in things; with respect to God, it is the expression of the Father's fullness of love for the Son in the Holy Spirit. The Colossians must know this. In the concept of this fullness, as it *pleased* the Father and as it resides in the Son, they should experience the greatness of him who fulfills their faith. It is not enough for them to see in Christ the promised Son of God, nor for them to recognize him as Head of the Church, as the One who exists before all creation; they must be impelled farther beyond all comprehension, in order to believe at least, if not to experience, the incomprehensibility of his unending fullness. Were they to try with their shortsighted intellects to establish who the Son is, they would continually be forced to declare in a human manner, "He is that, and so he is not this. . . ." If, however, they know that absolute fullness resides in him and that this residing belongs to his living, working being, then they really believe that he is exalted above all comprehension and description. They perceive that their faith at all times finds in him a superabundant fulfillment and that their love, however fervent, meets in him a yet greater love. His fullness does not stand in contradistinction to any void, because it is not the fulfillment of a determined quantity or a particular power of comprehension. It is fullness without antithesis.

1:20. *And through him to reconcile to himself all things, whether on earth or in heaven, making peace by the blood of his cross.*

From the perspective of reconciliation, the world has known three epochs: the time in paradise before the Fall, when harmony prevailed between Creator and creature, and everything was orderly and in its proper place. God was able to pronounce every single thing good, because it stayed within the framework of God's purpose, and he did not have to revoke his initial judgment. Then comes the era of sin together with the Old Covenant; the human race strays ever farther away; God grants them the promise of a new reconciliation, but they will not let that stop them; they wander on to the complete ruin of their relationship with God; they draw downhill after them even indifferent things in this worsening slide. In response to this, the Father inaugurates the third epoch: the time of a reconciliation that will last, even where mankind tries to break out of the relation of being reconciled.

God reconciles *through* the Son; he leaves the entire work of reconciliation in his hands: as the Son on the Cross commends his spirit into the hands of the Father. And this work is to encompass *all things*; it is to stand, unthreatened, over all, even over what opposes this work. Every man, everything is to receive its place within this work of the Son. For everything that happens is *ordered to him*. The ray between God and mankind is refracted by him as if through a prism. "No one comes to the Father except through me", says the Son, and this saying corresponds to the precise purpose of the Father, who wants to see every vindication accomplished through the Son. It is reconciliation in the broadest, most magnanimous sense: an epoch of new love, of heavenly love making a visible appearance: the Father delivers over to men his beloved Son, so that they, too, might love him together with the Father. So that they may be overcome by filial love and thereby be reconciled with the Father. All roads to reconciliation go *through him*, the Son, but he determines them. They are paths of love, pure and simple.

Indeed, the work encompasses *all things, whether on earth or in heaven*; reconciliation knows no boundaries of time or space. The *earth* includes everything that has happened on earth, *heaven*, everything otherworldly. In heaven, too, reconciliation takes place—whatever has turned its back on the sinful world makes peace with it—and this reconciliation, too, can happen only through him who was made man and through his Cross. In the Cross of the Son there is, so to speak, a double renunciation: he gives his blood for mankind; but in the same blood is found the power to reconcile the heavens. Every reconciliation with God is brought about through the Son and his blood, including the fact that the powers of heaven are reconciled in the face of the evil things that still keep happening on earth. The blood of the Lord continues to have even for the blessed in heaven the same strength as for those living on earth; no one can leave it behind or do without it. Through this blood that has been shed, those in heaven acquire an attachment to the world, which causes them to participate continually in the great work of reconciliation. However badly they may have been hit by evil, they do not turn away from it, just as God allows himself to be deprived of his righteous anger through the blood of the Son. God and his holy ones and the Son and those who dwell in heaven and sinners on earth and the dead in the nether world are in contact with this blood, and that is what gives it its actual and ongoing power to reconcile. It is always fresh and flowing, and so it is understood that the species of wine in the Eucharist suggests the everlasting reconciliation of the Father. If the Son in a manner of speaking gives himself away in the form of bread, which conceals his body—a gift from God to mankind —then the Father in a manner of speaking takes mankind back from the world through the blood, being mindful of the reconciliation that was accomplished once and for all. The sacraments signify, in common and in their concerted action, that the Lord lives within us; therein lies a movement, streaming back and forth, a twofold, reciprocal flow. (From this perspective, one can also justify the fact that it is precisely the priest who drinks the consecrated wine,[1] that the one who gives absolution should be the custodian of the Precious Blood, the sign that reconciliation has been realized. This is not to say that the priest is any more reconciled than the layman: both share equally in the effects of reconciliation, but the priest has the office of dispensing it in hearing confessions.)

---

[1] In the 1950s, when this was written, generally only the priest received the Precious Blood at Communion.

1:21–22. *And you, who once were estranged and hostile in mind, doing evil deeds, he has now reconciled in his body of flesh by his death, in order to present you holy and blameless and irreproachable before him.*

The Colossians ought to know how great was the transformation that took place in them. Previously they were not only *estranged* but positively *hostile* in their *mind*. They were strangers, since they were far from God and ignorant of his true teaching. They proved to be hostile when they heard about it but could not at first accept it. And this attitude, which characterized them as individuals, was at the same time a bond among them, so that each one could judge the other by himself. This interior attitude, present in their *mind*, drove them to *evil deeds*; the two inextricably form a unit, the fruit by which the authors of the deeds and the attitudes could be known. The Colossians must recognize themselves in this judgment of the Apostle and submit their judgment to his. In order to recognize themselves in this picture, though, they need the distance that reconciliation has gained for them.

But Paul does not dwell on this distance; he immediately shows the meaning of reconciliation. The Lord has redeemed them, *in order to present* them *holy and blameless and irreproachable before him*. The new qualities are dissimilar to the old ones already in the fact that they all have their fulfillment in the Lord, in appearing before him, in dependence upon him. Holiness is an attribute of the Lord; it is conferred by him on those who believe. And whereas the wicked deeds and evil thoughts used to make their perpetrators, the Colossians, known, now the holiness of the selfsame Colossians does not reflect on them but on the Lord. It has its meaning in him and its origin from him. By observing them, the world should be able to tell that the Lord takes his own seriously. And they should not only be found free of reproach for his sake but also be able through him to approach the presence of the Father, so that the Father may find in them this sign of sonship. Their holiness has this quality of reflecting the Son whenever they meet other people on earth and when they are presented to the Father in heaven. The Son has brought this about for them through his Cross; so that they need not be ashamed to bear the sign of the Cross and to acknowledge publicly their loyalty to him. He took this sacrifice upon himself for the sake of this sign, by which they are to be recognized before God and men as his own. The Colossians, like all who have been reconciled and believe, should feel obliged to the Son: to his Cross, to his blood, to his *death*. For what he immolated was his *body of flesh*. It was not, as in the Old Testament, the body of animals or the body of Isaac. When he willed to sacrifice, he selected his own body, his flesh in the most literal sense; in fact it was precisely in order to offer the most perfect sacrifice to the Father that he took on this flesh, with the intention of immolating it. He did it for the Colossians as well as for everyone else; the Colossians should feel obliged to him, and the thought that others who may not yet have heard have been reconciled should be an incentive for the Colossians to make known to them, too, the good news of redemption.

1:23. *Provided that you continue in the faith, stable and stead-fast, not shifting from the hope of the gospel which you heard, which has been preached to every creature under heaven, and of which I, Paul, became a minister.*

The letter shows now the portion that has been reserved for mankind. God has placed in his spiritual creatures something like a limit to his own activity, in that he has endowed them with understanding and thereby with their own power of discrimination, which enables them, in the domain of freedom allotted to them, to decide for them-selves. The decision that the Colossians have made in favor of the faith is not only God's gift, it is also their personal act and remains in this respect subject to pos-sible wavering. In the course of time they have to con-cern themselves with keeping their decision fresh. The decision reached in faith and for the faith requires rep-etition, simply because knowledge of the faith broadens and deepens; on the other hand, each new decision must be based entirely upon the previous ones; each new day, as far as faith is concerned, should verify those that have passed. Believers can be sure, then, of being without re-proach before the Lord if they only *continue in the faith* and are *stable and steadfast* in affirming what they have af-firmed thus far; if they only allow the faith, which they have freely made their own, to move them to reinforce it again and again. They have *heard* it as the *gospel*, thus they have received from the outside something that they were entitled to through the Cross of the Lord. The gospel was proclaimed to them, just as it *has been preached to ev-ery creature under heaven*, and it was communicated under the same conditions to which *Paul* was committed as a *minister*. The gospel appears here as the record of revelation, the objective good news about the unalterable fact of what the Son has accomplished; its effect is that the faith is kindled inwardly, but also that it is verified impartially and that men and women are made saints by it. It is a grace that they have heard the gospel and have accepted the faith; and now they must make their personal contribution through perseverance: by becoming what the servant of the gospel, Paul, admonishes them to be and, what is precisely the same thing, what the Lord through his sacrifice has bestowed on them in abundance.

And besides what the gospel is today, there is hope in it as well, marching forward with an increasing knowledge of what is yet to be, which is enclosed in the mystery of the Son, in his relation to the Father and to the Spirit, and which constitutes his life in heaven and eternity. This hope for the heavenly mysteries belongs inseparably to the faith because it is part of the gospel, something belonging to the mission of the Lord that completes by its strength whatever may be weak in the faith of the individual. The believer knows that the Lord grants this additional strength, that the One who has already granted faith through the good news will grant yet even more than the believer can receive, that in his words, above all in those about heaven, everyone can find prepared for him a fulfillment on the scale of eternity.

THE SERVICE OF THE APOSTLE

1:24. *Now I rejoice in my sufferings for your sake, and in my flesh I complete what is lacking in Christ's afflictions for the sake of his body, that is, the church.*

The disposition in which Paul lives is joy. That is how it is with a faith that hopes. And so Paul can *suffer* in joy as well. It is a consequence of the Lord's Cross that, in the Apostle, what is supernatural has prevailed over what is natural, faith over routine and joy over suffering. Not in such a way that he feels any less *in* his *flesh* the humiliation that he is subjected to, the pains and the afflictions, as though it were not actually an ongoing battle of the goal (joy) against the means (sufferings). On the contrary, he suffers the full measure of the sufferings destined for him, with an intensity corresponding to God's purpose, but he suffers in faith, which makes the final goal seem much greater than the means: the goal of serving the Lord. And so he rejoices in his service, even when it consists of suffering.

And since he suffers as an apostle, he does not do so in solitude but rather in solidarity with his brethren. Indeed, he suffers *for the sake of Christ's body*. For each person whom the Lord has chosen to suffer, he has set aside something from the profusion of his sufferings on the Cross, in order that the suffering soul might round it out and bring it to him as an offering, that he may suffer it not only together with him but as though in place of him, that he may bear it as a lot and portion that the Lord has explicitly left to him. Thus Paul's suffering is a suffering on the Cross, a suffering in connection with the body of the Lord, directed to him as is everything else of Paul's, but in the awareness that by sharing therein he anticipates and assumes a part of it that would be lacking to the Lord if Paul were not suffering it. It is a mission within a mission, a task within the task that the Lord has assigned to him. And Paul suffers for the body of the Lord, *that is, the church*. He suffers together with the Lord on the Cross and at the same time in the Church for her; both are found together in his suffering. And found together also are the suffering body of the Lord, the suffering body of Paul and the body of the Lord that is the Church. It is one single suffering they have in common, in which all is combined in an extremely concrete fashion. As the Lord took on flesh in order to die on the Cross, so Paul remains alive, in order to take part in this, the Lord's work of fulfillment. Here one gains also a new appreciation of the place of the Eucharist, which establishes the concrete connection between the body of the Lord that is immolated and the suffering of the Church, which dispenses to the individual saint the body of the Lord, thus making effective her incorporation in him. Two unities are made visible: body of the Lord—Eucharist—the Christian communicant. And: suffering body of Christ—suffering body of Paul—suffering Church. The two levels intersect. In every place where they meet—it is precisely here that Saint Paul is at his post—Christ's work of redemption comes alive in the highest degree; what he has done remains present there. His eternal will, to rescue suffering humanity through the Cross, works itself out completely. Every time there is a crossing at such a place, something of the absolute obedience that the Son accomplished on the Cross must be repeated. Then the unheard-of will occur: a Christian will be capable of working together with the Lord in such a way that the effects will remain completely hidden to him because, while suffering, he will be able to see everything only from the perspective of suffering (in which meaning and success are nowhere evident).

1:25. *Of which I became a minister according to the divine office which was given to me for you, to make the word of God fully known.*

It is no private assignment that Paul fulfills in God's sight; he was put into the Church: the Church must be for him just as real and true as God is truth; the Head of Christ's Church must be just as real for him as his body, the community. He is *a minister* of the Church *according to the divine office*, so that he represents a point of intersection, where divine commission and ecclesiastical commission meet and coincide; having accepted the two united, he also has to carry out both as a unity. He has been burdened with the Colossians as well as with the other communities. But since the letter is addressed directly to them, they must make the intersection real at this precise moment, without thereby excluding the others.

To make the word of God fully known to them. That is Paul's task: to bring to fulfillment the word that has been received, to prepare a fitting hearer for the word that has been heard, to arrange for the word, which has been understood by this believer, an audience with all the others, too. His service can scarcely be thought of as a matter strictly between him and God; neither can it ever be considered finished or bounded within the Church; as it draws ever-widening circles, it also draws the hearers of the word into service with him. Those who share in his task—and not one of his hearers will be able to say he is not called to do so—will themselves become new radiant sources of light and must take on obligations with respect to God and to the Church and share these tasks with others in turn. God's word, as the Church assumes a responsibility for it, remains until the end of the ages in a state of becoming. Everyone who comes into contact with it must collaborate in the fulfillment, just as Paul is doing. The word of God, with which the Son has identified himself, remains in human hearing a word that is always being fulfilled at this moment, because the Son as Word vis-à-vis mankind embodies the surpassing greatness of God. He gives himself to them in such a way that they must strive after him, fulfilling ever more and more what he alone possesses and manifests in its fullness. What the Lord is, we are able to approach through the gospel; in his fullness we can take on a task and fulfill it, even though in the presence of the Lord's divine perfection it always remains a task yet to be fulfilled.

Earlier Paul said that he fulfills in his body what is still lacking in the sufferings of the Lord; now in his commission he fulfills the word of God. This demonstrates again that body and commission constitute a unity of becoming and of obedience, a unity that is so clearly manifested in the Lord's gift of the Eucharist that the recipient comprehends how and where he must follow the Lord, indeed, why he was created to have a body. He should offer it for the purpose that the Son had in becoming a man. A human being is an irreducible unity; one cannot be a Christian in thought only and permit the body to lead a life of luxury. One can serve the Lord only with body and soul together.

1:26. The mystery hidden for ages and generations but now made manifest to his saints.

The word that was entrusted to Paul, that he might proclaim it, has a reality that can be described as presence, existence and quiddity (being so and not something else). But it is no less true that it has the reality of the *mystery hidden for ages and generations*. That does not mean that the present revelation of this mystery—the christological mystery of the Son in the Father—only now actualizes it. For the Word was with the Father in the beginning; the Son lived from all eternity hidden in heaven with him; he remained more hidden than revealed in the promises of the Old Testament also, concealed in the intentions of the Father, in the working of the Spirit, even where he seemed to emerge already, in the word of the prophets, which to be sure adumbrated/intimated a mysterious future but which, insofar as its contents were comprehensible in its time, remained narrow and limited. God wanted to keep the secret to himself, ready to be revealed at a later date. When God's Word becomes flesh, however; it discloses with every utterance, every miracle, not merely the will of the Father for the present, but also the design that he cherished from the beginning; it surrenders truths that only now dawn on mankind in their perfection, although they have long, from all eternity, been in the presence of the Father as truth.

And God has *now made manifest* the mystery *"to" his saints*, "among" and "in" those who are holy by virtue of the faith, whose lives are directed to the Son, whom he prepares and enables to understand the greatness of the mystery. Then they will no longer regard the faith as something constricted that for the time being binds them with heaven and the Church, but rather they will see it as the opening up of unfathomable truth from of old, which has possessed its fullness in God and through God. This faith, in comparison to the earlier sort, has such an incomprehensible breadth that there is no other way to explain it except to say that God the Father has thrown open the sphere of intimacy that joined him with the Son and the Spirit and has allowed the Son to come forth, so that the world might recognize the Father through him, has let the Son be the Way, the Life and the Truth for mankind, so that on earth the Supreme Being could be known. Now Paul and the members of his community can cite any word from Scripture whatever and thereby open up all the treasures of divine truth. Nothing there remains detached, questionable, foreign, isolated, inaccessible. Everything is found within the overarching context of eternal life: of that which the Father together with the Son and Spirit proposes, brings about and shares. And if Paul is supposed to fulfill the word of God, then that means he becomes the servant of this fullness of truth that pours forth from God. The fact that it is unveiled obliges mankind more deeply but also endows them with so much knowledge that from now on they can direct all their ardent desires toward God.

1:27. *To them God chose to make known how great among the Gentiles are the riches of the glory of this mystery, which is Christ in you, the hope of glory.*

The saints are now in opposition to the *Gentiles*, but not in enmity, rather in the unity of God's plan for salvation, which entrusts to the saint the gift he is supposed to present to the Gentiles. That is why the saints assume with the duties of their faith another obligation with regard to the Gentiles. God wills that the latter come to know *the glory* of the *mystery*. It should throw them off their course and confront them with something wholly New that awakens in them the thirst of an ardent longing. They should perceive it as *riches*, as do the saints, as even God himself does, and at the same time as *glory*. Something so glorious that man can only cherish a *hope* for it. It is not something that one can deal with arbitrarily, taking or leaving it at one's own discretion. It remains, even when revealed, the proclamation of an overwhelming mystery of God. So much so that the hope for it constitutes a part and a beginning of this glory. This is no groping about in vagueness, no turning to one side from which one can turn back again; this glory has an absolute character that derives from God himself. The hope of glory is synonymous with *Christ in you*. Christ

is not a greatness that can occupy a limited space within
Christians. If he is present, then he immediately extends
his presence and his claim upon them, just as hope, too,
can only be growing: it both promises and grants ever
more and more. No more Christ hidden in heaven, Christ
as mystery, but instead Christ as Someone manifested in
them. God creates within mankind the nearness of Christ
analogous to the nearness the Son possessed from the beginning in the Father. This is nothing fleeting, no mere
vision; it is a habitation and an abiding, and through this
indwelling of Christ in human souls the truth of hope is
ever more richly disclosed and developed and displays the
glorious mystery in its fullness. It is the Father's gift to
the world. When in the beginning he created the world,
he gave this just-created creature to man as a gift: he gave
the fruit of the divine act to the man who was created
in that same act. It was a gift that came to the man from
outside and that fulfilled externally the conditions the
man needed in order to live. When the Father gave him
his Son, however, to dwell within him, he gave him that
which God himself possessed from eternity, not a thing
created especially for man, but the mystery of the divine
fullness from the beginning in heaven.

1:28. *Him we proclaim, warning every man and teaching every
man in all wisdom, that we may present every man mature in
Christ.*

Christ is not only the hope of glory, he is the substance
of every word of warning spoken by Paul and the saints.
Therefore they can never move away from the Lord,

never proclaim a part of the truth without reference to him, never utter a sentence that could be understood in the same sense within the wisdom of other nations, unless it had a connection with Christ. For he is the touchstone and test of truth, in him truth is true; he is the Word that disposes each and every word that is proposed.

So on the one side stands Christ as the substance of these tidings; on the other side—*every man*. Every man who needs to be *warned* and who requires *teaching*, who has to experience *all wisdom*, not for his own enrichment, but rather unto Christ, so as to attain perfection in Christ. When the Son became man, he was a perfect man, Son of the Father in union with him, living and persevering in such a way that the Father saw his will fulfilled in him at every moment, in him who for the sake of mankind became man. And since the Son represents every man in the Father's sight, everyone is affected and embraced in this process; and so Paul can strive with some prospect of success to lead every man to completion. The apostles do nothing more than present the word, so that Christ may dwell in a man, so that a man may have placed before his eyes, not only an ideal and an example, but the living Son, who dwells within the Father and who wishes now to take up residence in the one who is coming to faith. Therefore the latter can venture to walk the way of perfection. The apostles, however, present the believer to the Father as one who, endowed with the Son's attributes, becomes through his indwelling someone who can look forward to completion in Christ.

Thus it is a twofold presentation: Paul presents to every man the Son, the One who became man; to the Father he presents the believers, in whom the Son dwells. In this twofold presentation, the efficacy of the Incarnation proves to be the fruit of redemption and of faith. The purpose of his coming is fulfilled through him in *every man*, and through *every man* this fulfillment is demonstrated to the Father.

1:29. *For this I toil, striving with all the energy which he mightily inspires within me.*

The relation of grace and merit, portrayed in the life of Saint Paul! He works at his God-given assignment, he knows it well, and he labors. And just as the knowledge comes from God, so too the power to carry on. It is the power of Christ, the force of his indwelling in him, which carries out this work together with him. Both are necessary, knowledge and power; both are the gift of grace. What Paul is able to do when he exerts himself physically and suffers sorrows, pains and deprivations is only rendering obedience in the paths marked out by God. Grace moves him, so that he can hear what the Lord commands; once he has heard and understood, though, Christ goes to work *within* him. Christ's *energy* in him carries out the task. He may well offer himself to fulfill the Divine Word on earth and to help complete what is still lacking in Christ's sufferings on the Cross; what remains decisive is that whatever he does is done in him by divine power. However reciprocal the collaboration may be, the indwelling of Christ and his working always has the upper hand; grace makes the work possible by preparing the believer and then drawing him beyond his own energies into its power, there to complete the work. If Paul directs attention to his special task, it is to demonstrate God's initiative and guidance, so that the Colossians, when they in turn have tasks to undertake in faith, will see how Christ deals with his own, what help faith has to offer, since the obligation is borne by the mighty power of the Lord.

GENUINE AND FALSE KNOWLEDGE

2:1. *For I want you to know how greatly I strive for you, and for those at Laodicea, and for all who have not seen my face.*

Paul declares his will, which he allows to come quite clearly to the fore; his will, however, derives from and depends upon his mission, and he seeks to integrate it in the Son, as the Son integrated his will in the will of the Father, which did not prevent him from allowing his filial will to be evident on many occasions. Paul *wants*, and behind this act of will stands the whole series of intentions that followed from his commission. He wills, and there before the act stands the possibility that he will realize his goal and thus effectively fulfill his mission. If his will is consequently to be characterized as altogether personal, still it really belongs to him only insofar as Paul lives in submission to the Lord and exercises his own will on behalf of the Lord.

His listeners should know how *greatly* he *strives* for them, and this knowledge should be beneficial to them. The insight into his inner life should oblige them, encourage them also and suggest opportunities. They should get to know Paul's life better so as to direct their own lives accordingly. Confronted with his struggles and cares, they should learn to struggle with him and recognize therein the struggles that every Christian takes upon himself in

following the Lord. Their understanding and their solidarity in bearing burdens can be a help to Paul, but it
must also bear fruit in *them*, until they are made worthy, in the same way that they show compassion, to have
compassion shown to them—until they deserve, by their
understanding, the honor of helping others to reach an
understanding. This means, finally, that they must become, so to speak, well-wrought work tools, cultivated
tillers of the soil; they learn so as to teach; they are re-
ceptive so that the kingdom may come; as "middlemen"
they build a thoroughfare between the Apostle and those
who do not yet believe, just as Paul is a "middleman"
between the Lord and the Church. Thus within Paul's
mission their own mission can be glimpsed, as Paul's mission comes to the fore within the mission of the Son,
without Paul's rank creating any distance between them
and the Lord or making access to him any more difficult.
To become a link in the chain means serving the Lord
personally by devotion, following directly after him and
responding to his immediate precept. This should be true
not only for Colossæ but also for those at *Laodicea* and
in general for *all who have not seen* Paul's *face*, who do not
have the advantage, as they receive his instructions, of
being able to picture him vividly. They know only his
mission in the Lord. The effect of his word, then, is not
bound up with his earthly appearance; the commission
he has received is a call to an objective greatness, and the
believers should get used to receiving the word of the
Lord through intermediaries just as fresh and new as it
was when others accepted it directly from the Lord. The
faith and the precepts are the same; human mediation and

the human community should not influence them in their essentials. That means also that the truth of the doctrine is as far above any individual's perception of its being true as the word to be explained is above the explanation and the word of the Lord is above the word of men.

2:2. That their hearts may be encouraged as they are knit together in love, to have all the riches of assured understanding and the knowledge of God's mystery, of Christ.

Paul goes now to his mission post; if the post does not make his mission coincide with the mission of the Lord, it still causes them to be most intimately bound together. He has taken an assignment in which the battle he has to wage becomes a means of instructing the faithful. Through his care they are to be strengthened: in that they are informed about it and follow his life and acquire some idea of his duties and of his obedience. He stands now at the point from which the fullness must shine forth.

Believers, before they attain the ultimate knowledge of the faith, should be formed anew by faith itself, by the working of the Lord within them. Their *hearts* should *be encouraged* and consoled, indeed, so intimately united with the Lord that his concern becomes theirs, that whatever makes him happy delights them, too, so that they receive consolations that are not of this world, that belong to his heavenly mystery, consolations through which he himself is refreshed and which already during his life on earth have come down from heaven and consoled him. The mere thought of being taken along and solaced in this way must have made their hearts tremble for joy.

Then they can go a step farther and *be knit together in love*: no longer claim any other place but the one assigned to them by love. The love of the Lord is a space where each one is touched by the same love, yet each one also reaches his own particular place through this love and can enter into a relationship with the others that is determined by love. Love causes the Christian to discover the attitude of allowing God to act in him: this attitude is an objective reality that comes from the Lord and confronts a person, who then subordinates himself to it in such a way that he renounces subjective self-assertion in order to permit love simply to work within him. It is love that brings him his task, assigns him his place and gives the power to satisfy obligations.

Having progressed this far, they must now attain *the riches of assured understanding*. This understanding is part of a sequence of events that began with consolation and continued in love. The latter leads to understanding—in superabundance!—to an understanding that surpasses the believers, because no longer is it they who want to understand, but rather an understanding above and beyond them is granted. The way of every Christian is meant to be an intensification that does not depend on him but is a grace. He stands under the waterfall of grace and has to let himself be sprayed on every side. That is how he becomes capable of performing the task that he is being prepared for, which he did not choose for himself, however: on the contrary, it lay concealed in the grace of faith. He cannot acquit himself of his task and cannot win the fullness of assurance and understanding except by devoting himself in love, which unites him with the others. The individual alone cannot suffice here, but the individual together with the others can. That is an image for the Church as the communion of saints, which applies also and precisely to the preconditions for understanding doctrine and to its dogmatic formulation. The acceptance of the truth that is meant here and the determination of its expression are not to be expected of the individual; they are a gift of grace that is granted to the universal community of those who are united in charity. In this process the Apostle is still at work as the personal intermediary, who now addresses, not individuals, but the community; he devotes himself in such a manner that his gift will be fruitful above all in those who are willing to walk the Pauline way of faith that he, Paul, has indicated. He stands there now as a cornerstone of the Church, for one moment emerging from the community, so that all eyes are upon him; but if they are to understand, in looking at him, then their glance must include the "let it be" of faith. Paul imitates the exposition of the Son, who became man in order to present and interpret in human terms what the triune God actually is in heaven.

This "let it be done" in the communion of saints, this fullness of assurance and understanding is used to come to a *knowledge of God's mystery*, a mystery that man's natural powers would never be able to figure out. Once Christians are transformed by the supernatural for this purpose, then it is shown to them in its fullness. It is really *God's* mystery: man perhaps has longed for it, in coming to the faith; his first faith had some inkling of it, but he was not yet ready for it. Certainly nobody can reach the maturity that would be required in order to be equal to the mystery. Despite this, God divulges it to those whom he has chosen and prepared, to those united in love, and it is not just any secret, but his ultimate, highest, most secret mystery. He does not want to feed his own with crumbs and fragments of a wisdom that would otherwise go un-used; he gives them the mystery absolutely, the greatest mystery, which has been jealously guarded from all eter-nity—namely, *Christ*.

Whenever believers experience Christ in the future, they will know that they experience in him the mystery of God. And that words such as "was made man" or "the Redeemer on the Cross" are parts of a whole that rests with the Father and that represents his highest possession: his Son. It is therefore understandable that believers had to undergo a complete transformation, so as to be permit-ted at all by grace to have any idea of what this is about. They have become, through the Son, chosen ones of the Father; the knowledge of the mystery entrusted to them too has made them proprietors of the riches concealed in the presence of the Father from all eternity. They are not only fellowmen with the Son, called by him and led to grace: they are now sharers in the mystery that belongs to the Father.

2:3. *In whom are hid all the treasures of wisdom and know-ledge.*

God has one mystery in which he has enfolded all mys-teries and which transforms them into treasures. As they are gradually discovered, they reveal themselves as *trea-sures of wisdom and knowledge*. The man who comes into contact with grace knows, in faith, that it springs from the Father, the Son and the Spirit; that grace, however, is not merely supposed to enrich him but should give him insight, set him on a new path, show him something decisive for himself and for the Church. He receives a mission. Grace never signifies something limited that finds in the graced individual its goal and its final rest; like a boomerang it wants to return to its origin. And the one graced is drawn into this source: God wants, together with him, to give more.

The works that the triune God has wrought in the creation and the redemption are full of mysteries for mankind: they disclose a little of the divine essence, but most of it remains concealed. The Father gives this concealed wealth of God over to the Son for him to manage and to dispense. The Son will not squander the Father's property—divine wisdom and knowledge—but will distribute them according to wisdom's plan: to those who, through faith and the effects of grace at God's bidding, are worthy to strive after these mysteries, to seek them and to discover them in all their fullness in the Son. God, as the eternally begetting Father, has given all his wealth over to the Son from the beginning. Indeed, in a certain sense he has *hidden* it in the Beloved Son, in order to forget, so to speak, how rich he is. When the Son then discloses these riches—still more, when he causes them to be disclosed through his elect, his chosen ones—then the Father allows himself to be enriched, for he gets his mysteries back. It is a kind of exchange of Christmas gifts that the Son arranges together with mankind. In every love there is an element of surprise and of wanting to be surprised; this, too, just like all other mysteries, was incorporated in the Son in order that he might display to the Father all the inventions of his love and give back to him the most secret, most genuine mysteries, those that the Father loves most, so that the Father might enjoy them as the gift from the Son. If the Son has always had all the Father's mysteries in his safekeeping, then he has not left them lying dry and fruitless in storage; instead, it is similar to what he expects of the servants who are supposed to make a profit on the talent entrusted to them. He can only do this by lending to the paternal mysteries something of the character of his filial love.

The Father has not made a selection and given some of the mysteries over to the Son and kept others for himself; he has given him everything at once, *all the treasures of wisdom and knowledge.* And when the Son reveals himself and gives himself to the world as a gift in faith, then he, too, does so without rationing or measuring out doses, but all at once, with everything that is hidden in him. In the very offering of himself he opens up his treasures completely. Indeed, to those enriched by him he offers this treasure also: together with him, the Son, to possess and to administer the treasures of the Father. He grants with his grace a mission as well. Paul appears as the principal catalyst in this transformation of the world: as the one who, by his devotion and his struggle, gains access for the faithful to all the hidden treasures of the Son.

2:4. I say this in order that no one may delude you with be-guiling speech.

Paul knows that since paradise, temptation has remained an ever-present problem. But now Christ is here, and mankind has been redeemed, and the power of God's word is in the world. Therefore Paul is taking precautions. He knows: the enemy will come in the form of words, in *beguiling speech*. He will oppose his word of enmity to the word of the Lord, leaving nothing undone in his attempts to *delude* us. That is the serpent in his new guise. The first serpent stood in opposition to the rest of the animal world, over which it was given to man to have dominion. The Evil One was this isolated form set against the other, far more numerous good forms. Now, though, word stands against word; speech against speech. And the Christians are forewarned; they know what it is about. From the fullness of the divine word they must draw strength to overpower the tempter's word. The latter will assume forms that really are seductive—will find arguments, furnish proofs that appear to enrich the spiritual experience of mankind; it will promise more on earth than Christianity can promise. It will force its way from the exterior into the interior, and so the interior must be armed. Paul's warning embraces everything that believers can still be susceptible to. If he mentioned previously every treasure of wisdom and knowledge, it was because Christians need them to fight against false knowledge. When the Son, moreover, with his death on the Cross, put an end even to his earthly life as the Word of God, his death was nevertheless only the prelude to his Resurrection, and that is also the resurrection of every Christian word that receives from the Cross the power to overcome, to make a victorious assault on sin, which was the purpose of the Cross. The power of the Resurrection of the Word is made available to the Christian, and not by chance, but rather because he urgently needs it, this power that is inexhaustible and that is permitted to remain among us because of its derivation from the Cross. The summation of the Lord's sufferings on the Cross, of his agony and his death, is found now in Christian doctrine, in the words of Paul, by which one can withstand every persuasion, see through the specious arguments and find the correct ones. Doctrine is the school of the believing soul and confers strength out of its own strength. Paul knows very well that his disciples, even though they have converted and have come to the faith and now feel called to be followers, are not yet sufficiently immune to temptations. And anticipating future temptations in a prophetic way—he speaks now at the same time from experience and from observation—he would like to cast out every one of them, so to speak, and conquer them through his word.

2:5. *For though I am absent in body, yet I am with you in spirit, rejoicing to see your good order and the firmness of your faith in Christ.*

Despite his bodily absence, Paul's spirit accompanies the community. For this to be so, Paul does not have to die or to allow his spirit to be separated from his body; yet even if accompanying the community spiritually does not affect the Apostle's union of body and soul, it is still more than a merely human phenomenon; it is a Christian potentiality, based upon a commission from the Lord and upon obedience to him, whereby the spirit, supported by grace, occupies itself with the matter of its mission. The Colossians, their conversion, their confirmation in the faith, form part of the Apostle's task. And this not just momentarily, not only when his thoughts happen to have a chance, in the midst of business, to turn to the Colossians, and certainly not only when the occasion arises for him to visit the community in person, but rather in a thoroughgoing continuity that suits the task and that, while being the condition of Paul's spirit, only the Lord himself can bring about. He, like most persons with apostolic commissions, must care for people and circumstances that are far removed from each other, and the fact that they are scattered threatens to endanger the power of the apostolate. Therefore God grants with the grace of apostleship something of the mysterious power of his omnipresence. The Son remains present to those whom he has sent, even to the end of the world. The Father does not abandon his children but accompanies them in a fatherly way. This attribute of the Father and this abiding in the act of redemption are a reality; the grace of a Christian commission remains in close contact with it. Therein lies the guarantee for the continued existence of the one Church that, transcending all differences of place and time, is all-embracing, because the great commission [cf. Mt 28:19–20] remains ever the one commission of the followers. If the Colossians or the Laodiceans had to manage on their own, without this contact with Paul, who is accompanying them, without the unity he brings about in his person (as does every commissioned apostle in his turn), then they would, infallibly, become eccentric in their interpretation of doctrine, go out on some limb or other, make compromises, expose themselves to the influences of the time and the place, give in to the allurements of their own reasoning, so that imperceptibly, perhaps, but unceasingly the center of gravity would shift, and after a few generations the doctrine would already have lost its unity, the Church—her true meaning, Paul's word—its urgency, and those who were commissioned—the very object for which they were responsible.

After Paul has brought attention to this unity of his commission from the Lord, which is not dissolved by his soul-body unity, he proves it also by showing what his spirit has experienced in Colossæ: *rejoicing to see your good order.* He really perceives this good order and understands it; he lives with it and sees its fruits, not weakened and diminished by distance, but present to him thanks to the workings of the living word of the Lord among the Colossians. He sees also the *firmness* of their *faith in Christ.* He sees their condition, then, and its development; how they hold fast to his teaching, just as he himself stands firm in the unity of the word. No matter whether they are near to or far from Paul: the unity is perceived. Not as something transient or insignificant, but as a reality revealed by God, which has its cause as well as its effect in the unity of the teaching that the Lord has founded. This reflects and corresponds to the way in which the Son, while dwelling on earth, remains with the Father and the Spirit, or to how, even after his Ascension into heaven and his return to the interior life of the Blessed Trinity, he remains on earth as the living, really present Eucharistic Word.

2:6. *As therefore you received Christ Jesus the Lord, so live in him.*

They have received the Lord: in his teaching, but also in the Eucharist. They have received his very being, which is to bring about their becoming. And as they have received him, so they ought to *live* and progress in him. One cannot receive him and at the same time develop away from him; one must remain in him in such a way that one's entire life takes place in him. It is not a development in the memory of him, a fading with the passage of time or the embellishing of a faraway ideal; it is simple progress—a walk with an unchanging Presence. To have received him is identical with being received by him. And each progressive step in the walk is just like the others, because all occur *in him*, whose reality does not diminish in power, since he remains all-present, eternal. Since the reception of the Lord is bound up with increasing knowledge of him and imparts each time a new fullness of faith, one can say that knowledge grows as one progresses, and the fullness of faith increases—always, however, and solely *in him*, in his truth, which has an unshakable objectivity; the reception determines the progress, but the progress on this walk, even today, never wanders from the reception. The Eucharistic Word is ever-now present, ever-now true, now as ever incorruptible, unfading, undiminished in power, so that the

progress of the final days can be exactly as powerful as
the first days of the walk, and each new reception is the
same as the first. Yet one is not walking around in a
circle but striding purposefully with ever-greater fulfillment, whereby the infinite worth and the actuality of the
reception are proved again and again.

*2:7. Rooted and built up in him and established in the faith,
just as you were taught, abounding in thanksgiving.*

This is the image of the Christian corresponding to the
image of the Lord walking upon earth. Just as the relationship of the Word-made-man to the Father and to the
world is expressed in Christian doctrine and offered to
believers, so they should make this relationship the pattern for their lives. They do not live in exile, in suspense,
in uncertainty. Their life is *rooted*, and that is the Lord's
gift, who makes himself for them the ground and soil
in which they can thrive. He is the firm foundation on
which their house can be *built up*. The Lord places himself at our disposal and thus becomes the prerequisite for
a Christian life, which perhaps in many aspects remains
concealed and withdraws from human sight. As one can
tell indirectly from the appearance of a plant that the roots
are sound, so too, from the fully developed life of a Christian in the world, visible to all, one can conclude that it
is founded on faith. The invisible prerequisite, the mysterious relationship of a man with God, demonstrates its
capacity to bear burdens by what can be built upon it,
what this man radiates. His life has, in prayer, one side
that is inaccessible to others, where his roots draw new

strength from the ground that is Christ. From that side that is publicly visible, however, everyone can tell not only that his faith is shining forth from its concealment, refreshed and strengthened, but also that his entire root system is in good order. The Christian life always has these two aspects of action and contemplation, one accessible and the other withdrawn from view; the two are to a certain extent subject to a law of alternating, rhythmic recurrence, but both are proved genuine insofar as they stem from the unity of the Lord, lead back to it and give witness to it. And so the Christian does not have to discover his way by himself, so to speak; he can walk according to the direction and the teaching of the Lord, *as you were taught.* And the Church is there to show him that these paths are fundamentally practical ones, to guarantee the unity of the hidden and the public sides of Christian life, and also to devise new forms of discipleship, all of which nevertheless have the common purpose of making possible the unity of Christian life in the individual member, because this member belongs to the unity of the Church, but also because this individual in following the Lord is a sign of unity in the Lord.

Therefore the Christian should *abound in thanksgiving*, should be aware that nothing is higher than thanksgiving. Thanksgiving that he is allowed to believe and that faith has brought his entire life into unity, that he as an individual at prayer belongs to the Church as a whole and to all her praying members, each of whom he meets anew in the prayer of the Lord. Every Christian prayer is in its sincerity a part of the Lord's prayer to the Father, part of the trinitarian conversation, taken up into the eternal purpose of the Blessed Trinity, which applies it and also uses it: so that the prayer might be purposeful, might spring from God's designs and correspond to them, so that it might release the Christian from the care of having to search in isolation, doubt and danger for the meaning of life. He walks a path that is shared, the Sonship of the Lord assures him again and again of his own status as a child of God; he is privileged to recognize, in the life led by the Lord, the one that he is to live. Whatever he may do as a believer, he can understand himself to be in the Lord, because the Lord on the Cross designated him as the one for whom he died, so as to present him to the Father. A new belonging, a new affiliation has begun here, so profound in its extent, so real, that nothing in the Christian escapes it, that every one of his concerns acquires a Christian meaning and purpose, so that ultimately he can only break out in overflowing thanks: for what is hidden as well as for what is public, for the root system and for what has unfolded from it and for every instruction received.

2:8. *See to it that no one makes a prey of you by philosophy and empty deceit, according to human tradition, according to the elemental spirits of the universe, and not according to Christ.*

Two worlds collide here: the world of the Lord, who from the very beginning possesses all wisdom and knowledge, and the world without the Lord, which is blind to his coming as well as to his essence and to any knowledge or wisdom. Paul has already treated the all-embracing position that Christ has taken toward creation. The Lord through his coming has fulfilled the Old Covenant, has poured himself into it as though into a vessel standing ready. Indeed, he has done the same with the whole of creation: he has endowed it with the purpose of his Being and has made this purpose comprehensible to creatures in Christian doctrine. And so the truth of the Old Covenant and the understanding of it, the truth of human existence before the Lord's coming, even the reality of the Father's creation in its entirety, have been brought to a new height and have entered a final phase, which could not have been developed from them alone. The truth of Christ is not measured by merely human truth, or by the standard of the world, or by the succession of days and the passage of time either, but has the immeasurable dimensions of eternity. Those men, however, who are blind to this truth set up a *philosophy* in opposition to faith, something that with some justification could have appeared as wisdom at the time of the Old Covenant, since on the grounds of tradition and on the basis of prophetic utterances and the entire Jewish world view many correlations could be discerned correctly. But even more was unrecognized or kept secret, and so it all remained only a preparation.

This wisdom has now been surpassed. It was correct insofar as it portrayed the primary elements of the world and developed approaches to truth that pointed toward the coming of the Lord. But since it did not recognize the fulfillment, it was bent into an *empty deceit*, it withered and died down. In this condition, nevertheless, it continues to have effect, because the men who still fight for it, imagining that in it they have grasped the sum total of wisdom, offer resistance in its name to the teaching of the Lord. They want to take the roots that grew legitimately into the tree of Christian doctrine and use them for another tree; they want to content themselves with what appears to the limited grasp of their reason to be the highest good. Because they refuse the fulfillment, the promise does not belong to them any more, either; they do not recognize in it any empty place that could yet be filled by God's action. They have so greatly underestimated what is possible with God that they refer it back to the horizons of their own wisdom, knowledge and finitude. They have closed off within itself what is unfulfilled and have turned themselves away from the fulfillment. They suppose they have understood God's wisdom and have monopolized it, but the God they represent does not exist, except in their philosophy.

Their thought is mere *human tradition* and has *elemental spirits of the universe* for its content. These elements exist, and what is thought about them need not be false. But it would have to be open to Christ in order to become fruitful in him. Without him it becomes sterile, untrue, nonexistent; to say No to the fulfillment stifles everything it may have had of a genuinely good start. The promises grow faint in the emptiness; tradition becomes meaningless; the primary elements of the world remain incomplete; wisdom loses itself in the complicated webs that it spins, which can no longer master the material of the living world, for the life of the world is Christ. They champion a life in a place where there is death; and the conquering of death by the Lord, which could give to the contents of their philosophy a new, divine, trinitarian meaning, is so sorely lacking that not a trace of this genuine life is left any more.

In the *elemental spirits*, which the Jews advocate, approaches to the truth could once be found. When the Jews are converted and acknowledge Christ as the Messiah, then everything genuine that they knew will be fulfilled together with them. The promises that seem to have gone for naught have found in the flesh and blood of the Son of Man their ultimate development, valid for all eternity. And a not very easy task has fallen to the lot of Christians, perhaps, if they are to discern and salvage what is right in the preliminaries that worldly wisdom is advancing once more. In any case they know that this piecemeal wisdom and these particles of truth find an overwhelmingly holistic fulfillment in the existence of the Son, which can never be sundered from the being of the Father and of the Spirit. Every truth of the Old Covenant, though, was bestowed with a view to this fulfillment, and so not one of them is useless. The Christian can go through the entire Old Testament and observe everywhere its fulfillment in the Lord and then, from this fulfillment, learn to recognize the fullness found in the Old Covenant.

2:9. *For in him the whole fulness of deity dwells bodily.*

Paul is presenting the theme of fulfillment in the Lord from a new point of view. Christ is God and man, but in such a way that this meeting of the divine and the human in him does not impose the slightest limitation anywhere. God is not in the least restricted by the Incarnation; it neither hinders nor weakens him; it does not put him in a state of unconsciousness; nothing is lacking to him of his divinity, his eternal life and omniscience. But nothing is lacking to Christ the man, either, as a result of his being God; he does not run up against his divinity as though encountering an obstacle to his genuine, full humanity; it is not as though he skipped right over finite human feelings, knowledge and experience and rushed like a stream into his divinity, finding therein a support for his existence that is unavailable as such to any other man. Rather, he is God and man in a union that leaves both natures intact and binds them together in their perfection, not making them merely run side by side. Only such a union can bring it about that *in him the whole fulness of deity dwells bodily*, that deity actually accompanies this human life and has a share in this genuine human experience. On the basis of the union of the two natures, the Son forever commends his human experience to God, that is, not only to the Father, but to the whole triune God, and thus it becomes God's experience in him. Yet he commends to God not only this man that he is; he also gives to all men who live by him, whether in his time or later, the fullness of deity in a salvific plan that all Christian doctrine sheds light on. Divinity and humanity are so intimately bound together in his being that they interpenetrate, with the exception of only those places where the fullness of one would constrain the fullness of the other and would cause harm to it. Aside from that, the two live in one another in a perfect vitality; God takes on perfectly the man united with him, and he who was made man is permitted to live in God. The entire earthly life of the Son is lived with the coming Cross as its goal, as a life, moreover, that simultaneously carries with it all created things, which from the beginning were made to return to him and which find their fulfillment in his life. He carries them in such a way that they participate in his death and his Resurrection. It must also be noted that a certain aspect of the experience of finitude has been affected by sin and that, if the Son is ready to experience this finitude and to bear it with us, he does so in order to become acquainted with human life as it is, but most certainly with a view to the redemption from sin that he is to accomplish. And this experience of a life that sin has made finite, that has fallen from its original perfection, that no longer corresponds to the original intention of the Father, is that much more difficult for him to bear, since he simultaneously has residing in bodily form within him the fullness of deity that opposes all that is sinful. But now it is the Father's plan that precisely he should bear this life and suffer from it more deeply than a sinful man could do; this with a view to the world's redemption.

If a Christian is permitted by faith to have a share of the fullness of the Lord, then for him that does not mean flight from the world and from human experience, or being closed off from everything that goes on in the world, or insensitivity toward its sinful condition; on the contrary, it means being more heavily burdened—and thus sharing the Lord's load—because the disparity between God's intention and man's alienation is more tangible to him. If one considers that, where a Christian has faith, the Son while on earth had the beatific vision of the Father, together with omniscience, a knowledge of the

Father and the Spirit, and insight into the Father's intentions, then one can see that the Cross was that much more painful for him to bear because the extent of the distance separating God from sinful man was perfectly plain on the path before him. Moreover, for him looking to God was the rule of his daily human routine; how much more incomprehensible and insupportable it must have appeared to him that men persist in their alienation. It follows from this that, when a Christian walks the way of the evangelical counsels in order to belong more exclusively to the Son, he too must always do so with a view to redemption, face to face with the sinfulness of the world, with the firm purpose of bearing consciously what the Son so sorely suffered under on earth. Purely private ascetical practices, which do not take into consideration the state of the world as a whole, would in the long run not be an imitation of Christ but would rather be opposed to his way of life. The person consecrated to God must suffer more deeply from the sins of the world, the more he has really commended himself to God; he does not have to concern himself about the suffering, it will be sent to him; yes, there is no question that it corresponds to his increasing participation in the fullness of Christ's life, which lives in him and is made actual.

The fullness of God that resides in bodily form in the Son is not visible as such to mere men. Still, it does not remain hidden; in every word of the Son, in his parables and his miracles, something of it is disclosed. It does not live in him in order to stay hidden as though in a vessel; it wants to stream forth into the world together with his human nature. Therein lies the lasting proof for the truth that he speaks; thereby his saying, "No one comes to the Father except through me", is also proved true in its fullness. Despite this, the fullness residing in him is not something that God might have created or selected specially for the needs of the world and its redemption and for the requirements of the Son during his stay on earth; it is really the infinite fullness of God with all the attributes of his eternity and abiding divinity, so that believers, when they observe the Son and allow the word to be effective in them and receive the sacraments, are in fact approaching the Father through the Church.

2:10. *And you have come to fulness of life in him, who is the head of all rule and authority.*

If the Son while on earth has the fullness of deity in bodily form, then he has everything: everything that is the Spirit's and the Father's, too, and there is no room beside him for any fullness that does not belong to him. The picture of the Son thus sketched is so tremendously great that a man who stands before it could feel neglected: If the Son already has everything, what remains left over, then, for him? Perhaps only things the Son cannot call his, because they are tainted by sin, things that because of sin possess a deceptive appearance of fullness and power? At creation the Father gave man dominion and power over creatures; when man fell, however, all sorts of opposing powers showed themselves; in many respects he was dominated by them and was therefore no longer able to exercise dominion easily; he had to wage an ongoing battle that often ended with his defeat. Then the Son appeared, and he was *the head of all rule and authority*. The power is not lost; he has it. When men sinned and disregarded its worth and threw it away, he took it to himself. And through him they receive it again in an unconquerable form. It is now in the Son as a sign of his divine fullness, and they are permitted in the Son to possess it. Faith is the condition for possession; love makes the title to it come alive. Through grace the Christian becomes a shareholder in the divine fullness of the Son's power, and thereby he also realizes what fullness of power was destined to be Adam's. What remained concealed in the time of the Old Covenant and was for the men of that era no longer an experience of faith comes once again to the fore with the appearance of Christ, but it is much more radiant than in the case of the first Adam. Therein lies not only the incomprehensibly surpassing greatness that sets the God-Man apart from the ordinary man; therein lies also a reparation that builds a bridge over all that sin has torn down, that removes the distance and fills the emptiness with the grace of nearness and heals the helplessness with the power of divine love. By faith in God's Word, which appeared in Christ, man can begin a new life, experience new joy, find new meaning for his existence; he sees the fullness of redemption streaming from the Son and coming toward him. By believing he receives confirmation of the fact that God's fullness was in no way diminished in the Incarnation of Christ; he is assured, rather, that Christ's dominion over all things, his principality in every way and his omnipotence stem from the fullness of the Godhead and bear its marks.

*2:11. In him also you were circumcised with a circumcision made
without hands, by putting off the body of flesh in the circumcision
of Christ.*

Relationship with God, the act of faith, entrance into the
Church and remaining in her is brought about through a
new kind of circumcision that takes place *in him*, in the
Lord. For every believer finds in the sending of the Son
and in his sacrifice exactly what he needs in order to say
Yes to the Father. If God's fullness resides in Christ in
bodily form, then it is plain to see that the human body
of Christ plays a particular role in conveying this fullness.
If it were otherwise, if in Christ only the spiritual side
were important, only the preaching of the word, instruction and admonishment, then God might just as well have
kept speaking through the word of the prophets. A similar argument could be made about the miracles. Now,
however, the bodily presence of God's fullness on earth
is bound up with the Incarnation. The flesh contains the
whole mystery. It is the sign, the sacrament that connects
men with the fullness of God. In the Old Covenant there
was *the circumcision made with hands*, before the face of God
and for him, as a sign of belonging to his chosen people. In
the New Covenant a person enters into Christ; through
his flesh, through his sacrifice, one becomes a member of
the living Church, belongs to God and shares in a Christian commission. The Son took on flesh in order to give
it up: the meaning of his life consists of *putting off the
body of flesh*, which goes much farther than circumcision
went, which can never be limited to a single act or to a
partial sign but which includes the fullness of what the

Son sacrifices for mankind. In giving us his body, both
in his death on the Cross and in his Eucharist, he in-
stitutes participation in his perfect deed. Everyone who
believes in him acquires a share of his death, in an infinitely deeper sense than that in which the circumcised
man received a portion of God. Christ's mission brings
forth from itself Christian missions. His death and his
Resurrection grant death and resurrection to Christians.
His putting off of the body of flesh becomes the putting
off of the outer man for the sake of the inner man; with
respect to the Lord, this is for the sake of his obedience
to the Father; with respect to us, it is for the sake of our
attempt at imitation. If we were to strive in doing so to
invent some sort of deeds that were not Christ's deeds
—for instance, a difficult martyrdom—then we would
deprive our deeds of contact with his unity; we would
be imitators without grace; our death would be senseless. Because he gave himself up for us, stripped himself
of the fullness of his human life for us, he became for
us the living sign and sacrament; and from this we are
enabled to receive the mark of life-despite-death, so that
the meaning of our living and our dying may be found
in him, and our existence may be fulfilled together with
and in his perfect fulfillment, and we may be sealed with
the sign through which we are recognized by the Father
as brothers of the Son.

2:12. And you were buried with him in baptism, in which you were also raised with him through faith in the working of God, who raised him from the dead.

The sacrament of *baptism* has in the New Covenant a spiritual scope that extends from the baptism of the Lord in the Jordan to his baptism of blood on the Cross and includes all of our Lord's life in between and his death as well. Yes, death is, in connection with the theme Paul is developing, particularly important; it is, to be sure, the new meaning of the circumcision and the putting off of the flesh, the sacrifice of life itself, but now with the inclusion of "all flesh", that of every sinner, because the sacrifice occurs vicariously. The sinner is buried together with the dead body of the Lord. He took with him into his death not only the two who were sentenced together with him but the whole of humanity, the redemption of which was at stake, so that Paul can regard the human race as *buried*: in the sense that all have experienced the end in him and with him, have come to an end of the liveliness of sin; they have not only died, they are estranged from the world in which they lived, and it has cast them off. And that is not merely wishful thinking, a product of the spiritual or moral imagination, nor is it merely the empathetic response of the believing mind to a consideration of the Passion, a subjective experience of accompanying spiritually the sufferings and death of the Lord on the Cross: it is objective reality that is the reality of the Lord, in which he gives us a share through baptism. The baptized person receives not only a juridical claim to enter the ranks of the Lord's followers; he receives in the grace of baptism the sum total of having been a follower, as it has been accomplished on the Cross. Thereby he has a share in things beyond his power to imagine, which in any case surpass the created world in its entirety and are things belonging to the God-Man. They can exist only in him; only through him and together with him can they be experienced. By undergoing burial he established a fact, the consequences of which God alone can survey, whose extent outlasts the ages, whereby every baptism makes this fact present again as a gift, as something already accomplished, already experienced, for the baptized person also, which then at some time or other in the course of his life becomes a living truth for him, breaks into his subjectivity and communicates to him some idea of what he is privileged to participate in.

In baptism, in which you were also raised with him through faith. The resurrection is the purpose of being buried together with Christ. It happens *through faith*. To have a living faith is to rise again in the Lord. Someone baptized (as an adult) without faith would not rise; someone who believed but was not able to be baptized would rise, and his faith would include the baptism of desire. It requires, however, all the power of one's faith to believe, not only in the Resurrection of the Lord, but in our own rising again in him as a reality that is established together with his Resurrection. Again: not in the realm of mere imagination and of argumentation, but in a realm of sheer grace, yet with complete objectivity, a realm that lives by the Lord and is communicated by him. It is faith *in the working of God*, in its effectiveness. God the Father has made his dead Son rise again, according to his plan of redemption: together with mankind. Ever since the Son of God died a human death, it is no longer possible to draw a line of separation between his destiny and ours. His life is also our life. But he does not awaken himself; in rising he allows the power of the Father to be manifested in himself. Precisely in this attitude of absolute receptivity he takes us with him: he brings us with him first into the will of the Father, which is to awaken us together with him, and our faith, fanned into flame by his grace, knows of this resurrection of ours. We know also that we would completely misinterpret it if we tried to explain it apart from the existence, the death and the Resurrection of Christ. The reality of God demonstrates itself in us, because the Son has taken us into union with him; it demonstrates itself to us, though, because we believe in him. The rising Son takes care in both respects— to the Father, who brings about the act of the Resurrection, and to mankind, in whom it is accomplished—to ensure that the consequences of his Incarnation are made visible in his Resurrection. These are accomplished facts, which we approach neither by weighing up our merits nor through intellectual speculation; facts that belong to the mystery of the Son in the presence of the Father and the Spirit. It is a sealed, divine, trinitarian mystery, in which we become involved because we have put the Son on the Cross, and because he has taken us into his burial.

2:13. *And you, who were dead in trespasses and the uncircumcision of your flesh, God made alive together with him, having forgiven us all our trespasses.*

There is a death that men die: the death of Adam and of the Old Covenant, which is a part of human existence and which is experienced in the first place perhaps less as a punishment than as the inevitable result of a sinful life. This death is the consequence of *trespasses* and the *uncircumcision of your flesh*. It is death that embraces both flesh and spirit as a reality, that unites the two things that led to sin and that have remained sinful; indeed, it is the very reality of sin. And now every Christian knows that not only has he deserved death because of his sins, but he actually was *dead*: if he were to look at the life of Christ, without the share in it that has been granted to him through grace, he would have to describe himself as dead. The life of the Christian is played out on a completely different level from that of the nonbeliever who does not belong to the Church, who has no share in the sacraments instituted by the Lord, who does not know the faith. With respect to the Lord, such a person remains the isolated individual who has gone astray and knows it, who loves sin and takes pleasure in it and does not wish to leave it. In the Church, the faith and the sacraments, though, the Lord has built countless bridges to reach individuals, to connect them with God and also with each other, and to let the reality of Christ flood in from all sides as new life. Anyone who does not close himself off from it must recognize that the life he lives by is the life of the Lord, in the manner, though, in which he has inserted it in the Church. The believer, however, is not hemmed in by the ecclesial community, by the details of the sacraments and the articles of faith, as though he were being nailed down to a particular place in church; on the contrary, he has all the room he could possibly need; he participates in the movement of the entire Church; he shares in the river of all the sacraments, in all the breadth of the Lord's truth, to which faith opens itself. The interior life of the one triune God cannot be reduced to a rigid geometrical figure; neither did the Son by his sacrifice want to force men into a mold. For living believers he has created a living faith; for those whom he loves he has opened up the realm of his love, of his Church.

Every individual would be dead without the life of the Lord. Each one would have reason enough to perceive and to grasp his own death as a relentless reality had the Lord not given life back to us, had he not *forgiven us all our trespasses.* He has forgiven us everything in order to give us back the fullness of life. And life after forgiveness has nothing left of the pettiness, the decay, the fossilization or the marks of mortality that went with the former life. It is a life that leads to eternal life, life from the life of Christ, who has forgiven, once and for all, and has taken mankind back in grace.

2:14. *Having canceled the bond which stood against us with its legal demands; this he set aside, nailing it to the cross.*

Paul does not enlarge on what this *bond which stood against us* contained or how long it had been in force. He assumes that the fact is known to the Colossians, indeed that every Christian, being convinced of his guilt, is acquainted with it. Of course it is not guilt because man knows about it; it is guilt in the sight of God, which he has taken note of and upon which he has pronounced his judgment. Therefore no one can decide on his own that he has a good conscience; no one can feel he is exonerated. Everyone knows that this *bond* against him is with God, who punishes the unjust even to the fourth generation.

Then comes the Son, who *cancels* this legal document filed with the Father, not just by throwing it away or declaring it invalid; he *set [it] aside, nailing it to the cross*, to the place where the Father is most sensitive, where the Son suffered everything for everyone. Paul describes in concrete terms how the certificate of guilt was nailed up; but behind the image there is a wealth of mystery, the entire love of the Son for the Father and for us. Our contribution here is only the sin, as well as our knowing about it, about the existence of our damnation. As for the Son's part, it now becomes evident how much everything corresponds to a predetermined plan. One must not picture his suffering on the Cross as something purely human that he endures passively and that issues in a valley of darkness where he is unable to do anything more; neither should the eternal attitude of the Son be imagined as the mere acceptance of the will of another, of the Father, to which attitude the individual words and deeds of the Son of Man then testified. One learns rather, from this image given by Paul, how much the Son in obeying the Father fulfilled his own will at the same time. He left nothing concerning our redemption to chance: by giving himself

over to the will of the Father, he firmly included everyone in his own will, in a will that had clearly considered
the entire work and had prepared it in advance. The Son
leaves to the Father the decisive hour; yet it does not find
him unprepared; he himself is ready from the start, and
he has taken all the necessary steps; we are included in
these preparations in such a way that the Son, even on
the Cross, does no more than what he sees the Father
doing. He has already nailed to the Cross the document
that accused us, and the Father will not be able to strike
him without hitting us as well in the way that the Son
willed, in the way that it is fitting for us to be represented
in his sacrifice, namely, through our sins. And all sins are
there, not one is forgotten, for the Son has taken with
him the Father's own list. If this bond were not there,
the suspicion could arise that the Son was suffering only
for the sins he encountered during his life on earth, and
the Father perhaps might be satisfied with that. As it is,
though, everything is lifted up into the complete objectivity of the heavenly perspective, of the triune plan of
redemption. The Son, so to speak, anticipates the Father
by taking the bond with him, and the Father appears as
though outwitted, and yet, on the other hand, the Father
does the Son one better, since the latter has to suffer for
the guilt of all mankind, for infinitely more than a man
could ever imagine. The Holy Spirit, however, sees the
measure of which both the Father and the Son have been
''deprived'' (the Father is ''deprived'' of it because the
Son fastens the bond of justice to the Cross of mercy;
the Son, because the measure of the atonement exceeds
human measure), and the Spirit makes himself the wit-

ness of this measure grown immeasurable. He watches over it during the event, so as to present it afterward to the Father and to the Son in the accomplished deed. Thus everything surpasses any agreement that could be devised, so that the grace, too, which proceeds therefrom for mankind, is greater and more extensive than anything a man could imagine to be the result of an agreement of his own devising.

2:15. He disarmed the principalities and powers and made a public example of them, triumphing over them in him.

The Son is one with the Father and the Spirit, and everything that belongs to the triune God belongs to him. In becoming man, however, he did not put his human possessions in opposition to his divine possessions. He is one Person in two natures, and if as man he dies powerless and rises again by divine omnipotence, then both moments make up his single destiny as God-Man, united with the Father and the Spirit and drawing into himself the destiny of the world, which he allowed to pass through his own destiny and to be stamped by it. God, though, is all-powerful, and the Son, who receives all power from the Father as his own, does not lose it during the powerlessness of the Cross. Therefore it is not true that worldly *principalities and powers* win power over him on the Cross. By allowing his powerlessness and his suffering to become an expression of his omnipotence, he robs the earthly principalities and powers of their power and dominion: precisely in the place where they are making ready to dominate, in keeping with their nature, they are forced into his service. He *disarms* them and brings them before his people, the believers, his followers; he *makes a public example of them* in the presence of the Church; and the place where he *triumphs* over them is the Cross. There he shows how he possesses power so thoroughly that he can even sink into powerlessness and still disarm the powers; how in the helplessness and exposure of the suffering and dying person, the all-prevailing power of the Cross is proved, in which the fullness of God's omnipotence dawns.

This mystery of his omnipotence and his powerlessness is displayed in *public* on the Cross. He owes that to mankind, to whom he recommends himself as the Way to the Father. He must show them the meaning and value of this way; they should not have to stop at truths that have no power to convince them and that almost cause doubt; they should see that they are led by the Son right up to the core of might, into the center of power: to the Cross. And by seeing him die and rise again, they themselves receive, through the mystery of powerlessness, a share in his omnipotence; where his mission is fulfilled, theirs has its source. The principalities and powers, which before were to be feared, are now *disarmed* in him, because in him they have been surpassed. From now on the meaning of the principalities and powers is the one that the Son has brought into the world from his unity with the Father and the Spirit through his Cross and Resurrection. This is not to say that all principalities and powers were evil before, or that their function has become meaningless in the future. But they are there to be seized and made part of a service, which is the Son's service of redemption offered to the Father. They belong to what the Son conquers, in order that his redemptive work might not end in darkness but will lead into the light; so that the Christian faith will be able to live by the strength of this light. The powers stand at the Son's service; he can use them as he wills: he can summon them and also empty them: thereby proving ever anew his oneness with himself as well as his union with God.

2:16. *Therefore let no one pass judgment on you in questions of food and drink or with regard to a festival or a new moon or a sabbath.*

Paul jumps, apparently with no transition, from the mystery of the Cross into everyday routines, from the summit of the New Covenant into questions of the old law. His intention is to draw the conclusions drastically. There are natural human needs, like food and drink. There are laws that God enacted in the Old Covenant and that were to be obeyed according to the letter, laws measured out for a humanity that had gone astray and was not yet really reconciled with God. And the Jews narrowed this measure down further, despite their knowledge of the freedom and glory to which they had actually been called, by drawing for themselves limits that were narrower and narrower, the better to control what little they seemed to control. The laws, in their pettiness and rigidity, in the sternness of their prescriptions, became more and more like prisons, which made anyone who wanted to obey these laws incapable of that higher and freer activity. And everyone could be tried and judged by others, by neighbors as well as by public opinion, by the people and by the assembly, according to how he kept or did not keep these laws. Feast days, but also the most everyday actions, like eating and drinking, provided the occasions for countless prescriptions.

And now Paul, not in his own name, but in the name of the Cross, the power of which he has portrayed, sets Christians free from these laws and legalities. They should not acknowledge the authority of this court any more, should no longer allow these standards to be imposed on them. And this means not merely in certain cases and with regard to certain people, but rather categorically never again. This liberation stands immediately beside the greatness of the Cross; Paul dares to make this jump into everyday routine so as to free Christians, that their entire existence may be drawn to this Cross, and so as to show the greatness of the portion allotted to the people of God. By this loosening of the laws to which they also were once accustomed, Christians are not left in a void but are brought to the place where the Lord is, where they are overshadowed and accompanied by the Cross, which alone makes them comprehensible now, which still is the triumph of the power and freedom of God.

2:17. *These are only a shadow of what is to come; but the substance belongs to Christ.*

The entire Old Covenant, with its law, its tradition and all that was laid down beyond that, is regarded as a *shadow*. The shadow was necessary: to announce the body as it approached; furthermore, to indicate it in such a way that those who wanted to believe could make ready. These things, precisely in their earthly composition and corporeality, were *shadows*, promises—which was no trivial function, for the outlines of the shadows were a forecast of the contours of the body that went with them, and by contrast they pointed out the body's density, its genuine and real character. And yet a shadow could not appear in time unless the body that went with it was already there. All through the Old Covenant the Son is already there, only concealed, standing behind the wall of his coming. But his shadow is evident and continually points toward him, without being able to divulge more of him than a shadow can of the body that casts it, a shadow that can point out reality only in an unreality. And yet in the Old Covenant there is a progressive revelation through the shadow, until suddenly with the birth of the Son the *substance* appears. Between the Old and the New Covenant there is no contradiction but, rather, surely an ascent by leaps and bounds from promise to fulfillment. Everything in the Old Covenant was an announcement; everything offered certainty about One who was coming, a certainty, though, that was never quite within the reach of the one who hoped.

Looking back from the fulfillment, though, we are amazed at the exactitude with which the Father painted in advance the Son's image in the law and the prophets, the image of the Church also and of freedom from the law. The Son will say of himself that no one comes to the Father except through him. Yet this means that, if the Father has drawn him in the Old Covenant, he now in his body on earth draws an image of the Father. In his body he gathers everything that was and what shall be and embodies the things past and the things to come in such a way that all the Father's intentions are made clear. If our Christian faith has to understand the Son as surpassing greatness, if every truth we grasp on earth is to be viewed as a particle of infinite, eternal truth, then the Jewish faith, too, rightly understood, can be open to the Christian one. The Jewish tradition and the law, insofar as they spring from the Father, will never deny the Son. That is why it is so essential for the Christian to concern himself with the Old Covenant, to be acquainted with Scripture, in order to learn more about the body of the Son, to be more fully initiated into his coming, to strengthen and deepen the foundations of faith in him. For all the Lord's words have their roots in the Old Covenant, just as his body casts its shadow back even to primordial times. The Spirit whom the Son reveals and the Spirit who points to the Father is the same One who also spoke through the prophets and thereby pointed both to the will of the Father and to the coming of the Son.

2:18. *Let no one disqualify you [of your prize], insisting on self-abasement and worship of angels, taking his stand on visions, puffed up without reason by his sensuous mind.*

If Christians understand how everything is shadow with respect to the body, then they find themselves as though in a contest for the truth. Tenet by tenet, from one day to the next in the life of faith, they comprehend more of the Lord's body. They believe because the Lord spoke to them and gave them his teaching as a totality; but also because they find throughout the entire Old Covenant evidence for the coming of the Son and for his truth. Thus they are completely attuned to the Son; they read everything the Father wrought in the Old Covenant and spoke through the prophets and enacted by the law as being directed toward the Son who was coming; for them it is a prologue to the faith. They themselves, though, cannot rest in their faith but must augment it in hope and charity by dedicating themselves in the same way the Lord did: increasingly.

Nevertheless, they do not escape the influences of the world around them; they might even lose their *prize* if they were to allow nonbelievers to set them back at the level of mere promises, instead of abiding in the revelation that proceeds from the body to the shadows. Under the guise of humility, pretending that they have neglected nothing, those nonbelievers could convince Christians that the wisdom of the promise is in and of itself already the fulfillment, something so profound it cannot be surpassed. They would merely have to step forward as prophets and initiates and claim to have had extraordinary *visions*, to live according to interior visions that contain the highest "truth" that can be attained at present, as if everything else, including the truth of Christianity, were nonessential, exaggerated and utopian. And yet this "truth" that is offered has been surpassed, in fact it can scarcely be considered a truth any more, because it corresponds to a bygone stage of development that has been transcended by Christ and that now lacks the vital connection of a shadow to the body. And since they do not want to deal with the living Lord, they deal with *angels*, to whom they show *self-abasement*, to whom they bow and dedicate their lives—angels that in the time of the Old Covenant might have been living powers but that are not so any more, but only artificially *puffed up* spirits, because the relationship to the Lord of all angels is lacking. In their worship of angels, they have a cult and a tradition that are without interior meaning; they serve an idea instead of a reality, an appearance instead of the living truth that God is. They persist within a framework that is no longer valid, because it is not the image any more that is present but the living body.

The Jew who lives outside of reality has to reinterpret the world according to the narrowness of his existence and of his awareness, according to his *sensuous mind*. The thoughts he contrives for himself, after shutting himself off from the grace of revelation, determine his attitude. This is *without reason*, because it tries to do without interior attentiveness to the body and consequently falls back upon itself and becomes a function of mere human thinking. For the Christian, this mentality can only cause harm, unless he with Paul sees through it as being idle.

2:19. *And not holding fast to the Head, from whom the whole body, nourished and knit together through its joints and ligaments, grows with a growth that is from God.*

The Jew in his apparent faith remains riveted to a spot at a certain height because he cannot bring himself to acknowledge the Lord as Head. Christ as Head possesses the body that casts the shadow, and this body is directed to the Head, is ordered, equipped and *knit together* with respect to the Head. The body, therefore, is not left to it-self and its own resources, as though enclosed and com-prehensible within itself; it does not begin a life of its own according to intrinsic laws and merely inherent pos-sibilities; on the contrary, it *grows with a growth that is from God*. Because it has Christ for its Head, it belongs to the triune God, obeys the will of the Father and is vivified by the Holy Spirit and by the working of its Head, the glorified Son.

God gave Adam a body having *joints and ligaments* and members arranged in a definite order, which complement and serve one another, each attentive to the purposes of the other so as to carry them out. The Son, too, takes on a body like ours, and so we recognize ourselves in him. But the growth of his body belongs to God. He lives his human life in the Father and does so for us. If on account of this the Jews do not recognize him any more as Head, then they deprive themselves of the growth that God grants us through the Son; they fall away from the living union that the triune God realizes for us through the Son. The growth of the Son in the Father has as its law complete submission to the Father, renunciation of what is one's own, constant self-divestment in the presence of the Father. The Son does not demand of the Father that he reveal to him his ultimate mysteries; he leaves to him the hour and the knowledge of it [cf. Mt 24:36]. The real life of the Son on earth consists in this self-surrender, and through him it becomes the real life of the Christian.

2:20. If with Christ you died to the elemental spirits of the universe, why do you live as if you still belonged to the world? Why do you submit to regulations [like those that follow]?

The Son, who lives from all eternity with the Father and the Spirit in heaven, takes up, in becoming a man, the *elemental spirits of the universe*, their tradition and their continuance. He takes the world as it is; he assimilates what he meets with, he takes the entire sin of the world upon himself so as to die on the Cross under its burden and for its atonement. Yet in this movement of drawing all things to himself, this gathering into his death, he takes all believers with him. He brings his heavenly way to earth, and in dying he goes back along this heavenly way with all those he has gathered here below, in his eternal movement of returning to the Father. Believers complete this movement with him, not as senseless freight, but as voluntary fellow travelers.

With Christ they *died to the elemental spirits of the universe*, because they are returning to the Father with the Son who has died—to heaven, which signifies the truth of the triune God. In his death, which by his redemptive act he has made theirs as well, they turn their back on the world. They do not belong to it any more; through this death they have become his brethren and are permitted to walk with him toward eternity. They cannot simultaneously travel two ways, continue on earth and at the same time return to heaven. They have become a part of the Lord's decision not to leave the Father while on earth; they are now already pledged to heaven, so much so that it has become their home. They are so by virtue of death, suffering and renunciation. The *elemental spirits of the universe* can no longer fetter them; Christians can no longer praise them as the highest or allow themselves to be tied down to their earthly abode while their soul already has its dwelling with God. Therefore they must learn to shake off what has become superfluous, so as to devote themselves to the one thing necessary. To hold fast to earthly elements and to die to them: that would be a spiritual contradiction. To follow the one commandment of divine love and to cling to the thousand human *regulations* would be one also. Present reality is for them the triune God. And the elemental spirits have become history and unreal. They live in hope, that is to say, in the future that belongs to God.

2:21. *"Do not handle, Do not taste, Do not touch."*

These are instructions of a purely negative sort, which, however, are not from Christ but are proclaimed by the world. When the Christian lives in the world as someone who is not of the world, then he does not flee the world, he does not conceal himself, but, on the contrary, he is open to and aware of what passes for truth in the world, what his fellowmen are entitled to expect of him as a man, but within a greater awareness found in God. The Christian understands his task in the world as a function of the Son's mission. To put it even more personally from the individual's perspective: whatever he undertakes he will submit to a constant evaluation by the word of God. In this way he cannot regard abstaining from some worldly things or other as the ultimate wisdom. That wisdom is, rather, devotion and obedience; something he himself does not have to devise and that he should not try to work out as a set of rules for his particular use. He does not have to imagine every case that can occur in the world, as it would apply to himself, in order to be more capable of responding correctly. Instead he knows as a Christian that his dedication of his entire life, and every partial response within it, are contained in the response of the Son in the presence of the Father; that he has only to devote himself to the Son in order to walk the right path; that in addition to that he must follow the great directives that the Head has given to the body, the Bridegroom to the Bride, so as to remain within his mission. In doing this he will always be conscious of the distance that separates him from the Head, but that will spur him on to devote all of his attention to his mission in light of the Son's mission. He will put up with practical and concrete directives, but only insofar as they are consistent with an ever-greater love for the Son and foster it; even more precisely: insofar as they are evidently commanded by the greatest commandment of love. He will not, in the name of Christian freedom, haughtily resist every directive but will meekly submit to everything that pertains to charity, which also allows his fellowmen to love more. Everything that is prohibitive, restrictive and negative will become meaningful as a partial realization of the positive commandment; not in and of itself, but in God; not as a command from the world for the world, but as one sent from heaven for a world that should always be more and more open to heaven.

2:22. . . . (referring to things which all perish as they are used),
according to human precepts and doctrines?

The rules: Don't handle, Don't taste, Don't touch, per-
tained to things that are for men's *use*, that are meant to
sustain life. They fulfill their purpose when they are used
and consumed to help someone keep body and soul together and satisfy his human obligations. They are there
for man's sake and serve him while he serves. They are
good precisely in attaining their purpose, by being assim-
ilated into the life of man. Their significance therefore is
secondary. Everything would be turned upside-down if
man were to construct a doctrine in which these things received primary importance, if, for instance, it were someone's purpose to exercise his will by renouncing these little things, so as to be equipped for greater causes. God lifts
man beyond such a merely human, immanent religion;
by grace he makes him qualified for eternal life, and by
virtue of this predestination for eternal life, which is the
primary thing, the will of the believer can be fit into the
will of the Son, his obedience can become an expression
of God's love for mankind and, in response to that, of the
love of mankind for God. Human precepts have meaning
only within this great arrangement. It would be wrong-
headed so to narrow down the nature of evil and good
that it could be discerned only by reference to worldly
things, while simply ignoring God's decision about what
he regards as evil and good. The Christian lives in the
world within a framework provided by the ordering of
the world to the Son.

2:23. These have indeed an appearance of wisdom in promoting rigor of devotion and self-abasement and severity to the body, but they are of no value in checking the indulgence of the flesh.

The life of man even within the world can be divided into different levels, corresponding to higher and lesser values, so that a person must renounce the one in order to enjoy the other more plentifully, or he relinquishes one work so as to accomplish another better. The thing he renounces will always be for him the less valuable. He can construct an entire system of such priorities and corresponding renunciations, which appears so intrinsically well-balanced and defensible that the total significance of all these values and all this self-discipline remains at first concealed—that is, that the shadow is taken here for the body, the appearance is mistaken for the truth. *These have indeed an appearance of wisdom*, because it is so subtly contrived and because the interplay among the various levels is so smooth. Man attains thereby a *rigor of devotion*; he follows rules that he has imposed upon himself in a cult of his own choosing; he does this in *self-abasement* that gives him an appearance of humility; with *severity to the body*, in a hard ascetical discipline. Yet this asceticism is not part of the Lord's arrangement but only serves ultimately to *indulge the flesh*. The carnal man renounces one thing so as to derive that much more enjoyment from the other. In such a system there can be so much that is true (which stems from the truth of the Christian life) that a test is indispensable for discernment. If the whole thing can be directed to the Lord, then that must also be true of all the precepts and renunciations in it. If it is incapable of this, then it remains sterile. All the precepts of Christian doctrine are fruitful. Not in such a way that they must always bear fruits that are empirically observable, but theirs is the promise of fruitfulness in the Lord, and if God wills, he can reveal something of it to us. It would be foolish to want to judge the fruitfulness of heaven from an earthly perspective, since we lack the standards and procedures for doing so; we just know in faith that nothing can be more fruitful than heaven. Whatever on earth contributes to the fruitfulness of heaven is *merit*orious insofar as God grants to man by his grace the possibility of genuine participation. If this participation in grace is lacking, then there is no *value*. And the ascetical system becomes an illusory half-truth without the fructifying power of Christian life.

LIFE FROM CHRIST

3:1. *If then you have been raised with Christ, seek the things that are above, where Christ is, seated at the right hand of God.*

The Resurrection of the Lord is an event that Christians know by faith and that is presented to them in such a way that they are continually urged on from understanding to a state of not understanding any more, from an almost corporeal grasp of the event to an intellectual condition of not grasping any more. It is not the kind of event that would mean for them a conclusion, in which they could be so much at rest that it would relieve them of any further questions. Every time their thoughts are occupied by the Resurrection, they stumble upon something unexpected, something new, that shows to them in a different light the relation of the Son to the Father and to the Spirit.

But *now* Christians have been *raised with Christ* and have been drawn with him into this incomprehensible event. They cannot regard the Resurrection as a truth that is played out apart from themselves; they belong to it, they too bear this fruit, even where their human spirit is completely at a loss, having been hurled, as it were, into such an extravagant situation. They must grow comfortable, not only with believing in the Resurrection of the Lord, but also with admitting as part of their faith their resur-

rection with him. The objection that this truth is too supernatural and incomprehensible for them is not allowed.
Starting from the opaque fact itself, they should go on to
investigate its consequences: that is to say, *seek the things
that are above.* It is not a matter of merely considering the
infinite; rather, it results concretely in assiduous effort.
And *above* means: *where Christ is, seated at the right hand of
God.* Their "resurrection with him" sends them on a tra-
jectory, on which they must catch up with their task and
let their co-resurrection develop into a co-responsibility.
Taken up into the heavenly things of the Son, they have
good reason to strive unceasingly for these things. It is
their concern that the Son sits at the right hand of the
Father. The picture that the Son gave to them at his Ascension, the sight of him being carried off into the air
and concealed in the cloud, should be for them a lesson
in understanding the integral meaning of his movement
to the Father. The movement of the Ascension must become for them an embodiment of their existence. And
the more the Son assigns them to this world with a Christian mission, the more they belong to the world of the
triune God, of the things that are above, the more they
take part in the movement of the Son to the Father and
in the enthronement at his right hand.

3:2. *Set your minds on things that are above, not on the things
that are on earth.*

At the creation, God called the earth into existence as
something different from heaven, but that did not cause
it to be anything other than good. And God made a gift

of these earthly things to Adam, so that he might rule over them. His relation to them was clear. Sin disturbed it; something of Adam's sin entered also into his relationship with things. The Son, in redeeming the world, did not simply restore the old order but took mankind and earthly things with him in a new movement toward the Father, and Christians have to fit themselves into this movement. They must lift their minds away from the narrowness of the world into the freedom of the Son and rejoice in what gives him joy. What he has at stake in his life should also fill theirs. The indivisible decision to walk the way of the Son contains within it an indivisible renunciation as well: a turning aside from all thinking that is incompatible with the mind of Christ. This is not case-by-case renouncing, progressively, in installments; the Christian mind is no longer made for the narrowness of the Old Covenant or for the narrowness of the world. It participates in all of the breadth and endlessness that God is opening for it in heaven, a heaven that no longer stands unapproachably and frighteningly high above the earth, but one rather in which the Son is seated at the right hand of the Father as one of us. In the New Covenant it belongs to the experience of faith that the Son is risen from the dead and has taken us up with him to the Father.

3:3. *For you have died, and your life is hid with Christ in God.*

The extent of this new life can be fathomed only through death. And every believer must know that he has died. One must come so close to the Lord that his death is experienced as one's own. And this, not in some act of imagination, but in the absolute truth of the Cross. As the Son takes man with him into the Resurrection, so he takes him into death, so that he might free him from his sins. Man's power and will, his being precisely as he is, are broken by the acceptance of the Christian faith—even more than broken: condemned to death. The execution takes place with the acceptance of the faith. As long as man regards the life of Christ as the fate of an individual in the history of the world that led to a crucifixion and a resurrection, he remains, with respect to the truth, in a condition that may content his imagination and his inclination to speculate and contemplate but that closes him off from any access to faith. For faith means having died together with the Son of God. And this is accomplished, not at the wish of the believer, not through some special intellectual attitude, but rather by the power of the fulfillment of the Father's will by the Son. When the Father looks upon the Son who has died, he must be able to see in him also the Christian who has died. The fact that the One who is sent allows his will to be broken in death for the sake of those who will follow should not be an exception: such a death is the norm for all, the duty and the grace of everyone called by the Lord to faith. This is expressed by Saint Paul's statement: "It is now no longer I who live, but Christ who lives in me."

The Lord has *died*, and we with him; and the life we lead in faith—the life of the elect, of those commissioned, a life of attempted obedience—is *hidden* in the Lord himself, so that the individual will have even less knowledge of his hour than the Son did. Yes, tomorrow and everything in the future is hidden from him, because they are located within the mystery of the Son's hiddenness. We do not live like marionettes, wrenched about at someone else's will and pleasure; we live as those who are alive with the life of the Lord, as those to whom faith gives the ability and strength, together with him, to do the will of the Father. This is the primary life that God had intended for man at creation, life directly out of the Father's hand, now restored through the death of the Son. A life in complete submission, as accomplished by the Son, to the will of the Father.

If even the life of the Son, who indeed was perfectly obedient, remained hidden in the Father, then we certainly will not want to make any claim to knowing our life in God or surveying its direction, its phases and its steps. We will much rather give thanks that ours is fulfilled and preserves its meaning by the fact that the Son is seated at the right hand of the Father and that our eternal life is made possible through the surrender of his life.

3:4. *When Christ who is our life appears, then you also will appear with him in glory.*

The Second Coming of the Lord in glory is an event that means far more than the believer knows. Christ will appear as *our life*: that is the definition of him that Paul gives here. A life that holds within it our life and the life of all. A Yes that includes every Yes in heaven and on earth. What we usually call life is the passing existence of individual creatures that are heading for death: plants, animals and men. But all these lives taken together would not nearly amount to the life that Christ is; for in him is the fullness of eternal life, which is distinctively his with the Father and the Spirit and which he communicates to us. That he is *our life* does not mean that it is in any way restricted but rather that our life is transposed into his, what is human into what is divine, something fleeting into the eternal. Furthermore, Christ, in taking up our life, does not drown it in his immensity; at his appearance *you also will appear with him in glory*, each at the place God assigns to him, as is fitting for the manifestation of his glory. This is the glory of the Father, of the Son and of the Spirit, and hence it exceeds all imagination. Within it there is place for nothing but glory; no comparison is possible, no limitation. And we, who know our limits and our failures and our sins, we mortals, to whom tomorrow always seemed uncertain, are permitted to be present in the middle of this glory, without darkening the picture, but rather so as to complete it, so as to receive back what we regard as our life, now transposed into the fullness of the Lord. The brilliance of this revelation exceeds every power of vision. Previously we knew by faith that the risen Son sits at the right hand of the Father. But now his glory is no longer separate from our world; it is revealed in such a way that it encompasses us with it, so that we make up a part of it. If beholding the Cross with faith was for us an experience of being taken with the Son into the death of redemption, then our experience now is of being taken along into glory. He leads us into a kind of sharing that is the counterpart to his earthly sharing in our sins. He took what is ours in order to grant us what is his.

3:5. Put to death therefore what is earthly in you: immorality, impurity, passion, evil desire, and covetousness, which is idolatry.

Man's *earthly* life is caught between birth and death, and the reality of death became more and more oppressive in the course of the Old Covenant; it fell like a shadow over all of human life. But now Christ has taken on our life and has given us his. His birth becomes the entrance of eternal life into time, and participation in this birth becomes for believers participation in the life of the triune God. The face of death is transformed, too, since the Lord uses it to detach man from his sins. And believers receive the power to cooperate in their own lives in this detachment. They can doom to destruction, *put to death*, the bad things that still remain: sin, temptation. They can do this by the power of the Lord's Cross, which has accomplished this detachment, but also by the power of his new life. The life of faith is life pure and absolute, with no admixture of death. Death stands outside of it. Temptation can be overcome; sin can be confessed; evil can be recognized by faith as that which is directed against the faith. Paul counts off, one after the other, the sins that man can go on committing in his members— sins, however, that he can also put to death in his spirit of faith. And this is what he should do. He should recognize for what they are this *immorality and impurity* and all the things that could separate him from the Lord, and he should fight against them with the strength that comes from the grace of our life in the Risen Lord. The Cross did not simply blow sin away; rather, it furnished believers with all possible weapons against it. The Lord has made the decisive move, and he offers the strength of his decision to Christians as they make decisions. With this strength they can kill, uproot and destroy. A decision for the faith is not only a positive decision for the Lord but also a negative decision of turning away from sin. One glance at the Son, who said: "Not my will, but yours be done", and the Christian who is being tempted will understand that overcoming evil is required by obedience to God.

And covetousness, which is idolatry. All the vices Paul enumerates are capable of imprinting upon man an image that is not the image of God. Man cannot bear both images at once. The fact that God makes man to his image and likeness establishes a living relationship between them, in which God's surpassing greatness and glory illuminate the creature (the copy), and man, therefore, must worship the Archetype. When sin, however, is held up as an archetype that presents itself to man's imagination and attracts him to conform to it, then the result will be a perverse kind of worship: *idolatry.* In man's lust, in his *passion and evil desire*, it has come to light whom he actually serves.

3:6. *On account of these the wrath of God is coming.*

God had established an unconditional relationship between himself and the creature; the Son has reestablished it by the definitive character of his decision for the Father. Without changing his eternal relationship to the Father, he became man, lived in that relationship and took humanity up into it also; the Father can observe the world now through this relationship. But when men commit idolatry by enslaving themselves to their evil desires, then they construct an antiworld opposed to the Son's world of redemption, a world that negates the eternal decisiveness of the Father and the Son. That provokes the wrath of God: the wrath of the Creator, but also the wrath of the Father. Heaven turns in wrath against the earth. When the Son instituted the sacrament of reconciliation, he granted his own forgiveness on the Cross, but also the forgiveness of the Father, on account of the Cross, and that of the Holy Spirit, who causes grace to become effective in souls. All three acts of forgiveness constitute a unity in God's unique economy of grace, which is for the world a sign of the trinitarian unity. The man, though, who persists in the idolatry of his vices does not want to be forgiven, does not want the Son to have suffered on the Cross for him. He does not want to bear the sign of the Son, by which the Father can recognize him as one redeemed. So nothing is left but wrath, a wrath that is mightier than heaven and earth because it has the power of divine omnipotence. Everywhere it uncovers the idolatry, the constantly reconstructed yet distorted image of true worship. God sees not merely the sinner's back, his turning away; he sees the disfigured face, the desecration of the image that the Son *is* and that he wanted to produce in man. Only after God in the greatness of his wrath has destroyed the idols in a man is there room available again for his mercy. But for one moment the full weight and the full seriousness of the wrath must be made evident.

3:7. *In these you once walked, when you lived in them.*

There is life, and there is the path that one walks through
it, the state of being and the kind of development therein
that do not lead out of it. Whoever lives in sin also walks
in it, he is accompanied by sin, he cannot put it aside
from time to time; he cannot habitually rest in it and
while there undergo a transformation and discontinue
the sin, as one takes off an article of clothing that is not
needed at the moment and puts it aside for later use. The
spiritual environment accompanies the traveler along the
path. That is the most serious thing about sin: that, once
chosen, it remains constant and sticks to the sinner. Unless help comes from outside, from above, unless he receives grace, man cannot get rid of it. If Paul juxtaposes
life and conduct in this way, it is because he wants to
demonstrate the power of grace without mentioning it
here. If the Colossians have converted and have chosen
Christ once and for all, then they have chosen an efficacious, efficient Christ, who in his Church has instituted
everything necessary, not merely to prepare the way for
grace, but to have it take effect. Before they came to the
faith they were in sin, and whatever they tried to do,
they could not free themselves from it, whether because
they did not clearly perceive the state they were in or
because, despite the realization, they were quite content
in it. Sin is so multifarious that it can always dazzle with
new images, offer or pretend to offer new conditions to
beguile man's boredom, so that he pays more attention to
himself than to the sin, is concerned about walking new
paths, all the while not noticing that he is going around

in a circle and has not progressed at all beyond his former state. The Colossians must recognize that they were
once provoking the wrath of God, see a new reason to
give thanks in the fact that God rescued them from that
situation, and be on guard against returning to the region
of wrath. The wrath of God is not something hypotheti-
cal; it is real and has its place, and that is precisely where
the Colossians were before their conversion. From the
perspective of the faith in which they now live, they can
gauge what the wrath of God was like. Faith is needed in
order to have an inkling of divine wrath; in a sinner's eyes
he covers himself with his sin; the sinner can no longer
distinguish what is God's from what is his own, therefore
he has also lost the courage to look for a way out of sin
and out of the wrath of God. The separation from sin and
wrath is already a work of grace. As long as he lives in his
sin, actually, the sinner will always excuse himself. Only
when he receives the grace not to do it any more can he
realize that he deserves God's wrath, but precisely in this
realization he is permitted to lay hold of grace. Whoever
acknowledges guilt leaves the wrath of God behind.

3:8. *But now put them all away: anger, wrath, malice, slander,
and foul talk from your mouth.*

The instructions that follow now are expressed in the
imperative, because the Colossians should have arrived
at the insight through what Paul has said. He enumerates
the things they should put aside, and each term carries
the full weight of sinfulness. No pretexts are possible.
Every word says: A sin is a sin; every word is intended to

make their conscience more keen. Light is thrown on the guilt; excuses are cut off. The sins enumerated all revolve around the word, around the expression of an interior attitude. Of an attitude against charity that acquires a contagious character through the spoken word. And now sin, the vicious circle of the state and the conduct, the inseparability of sin and sinner, manifests itself in a new light: in human utterance it gains the sinister power of drawing others into the same state: of hostility, slander and lying. And not by accident does Paul mention *anger* first, because previously he has characterized the wrath of the Father, and now he wants to highlight, though enigmatically, the Son's character as the Word, so that the sinner's misuse of the spoken word will appear that much more dreadful. The way leads from the righteous anger of God to the love of the Son and to his being and conduct as the Word of God, which contrast with the state and conduct of the Colossians who are in sin. And now, as believers, they have command of the Son's word, which revealed itself for them and suffered for them on the Cross. Their abuse of the word should seem to them in this light even more shameful. Just as the Son never bargained but did everything he did wholeheartedly: Incarnation, sacrifice, suffering and death, so too believers should never try to compromise with the word but should strive in all things for authenticity. Putting aside what is shameful, they will make all the room they have available to the genuine Word, the Son.

3:9. *Do not lie to one another, seeing that you have put off the old nature with its practices.*

Conversion takes place in two phases: turning from and turning to; renunciation and acceptance; No and Yes. The No is portrayed here as the stripping off of the *old nature*, a process that does not allow for any subsequent lie. For a fundamental No has been spoken against every sin. The old self that has been put aside is no symbol, no idea; it is sinful man considered with all his actual and possible deeds, one of which is lying. Through this decision those options have been excluded: what has been cast off is not worn again. There can be no more flirting with it, for that is the epitome of things displeasing to God. There are no clauses in the contract that permit someone who has converted to continue residing in a few rooms of the old building or at least to occupy them again during certain seasons and hours.

3:10. *And have put on the new nature, which is being renewed in knowledge after the image of its creator.*

The No of renunciation immediately leads to the Yes of acceptance. There is no empty space between them; what was put aside is transformed without a break into what is freshly put on. Man is made new. Not merely for the sake of transformation, but because *the image of his creator* emerges, the imperishable, unalterable image that is new for the man who is turning away from sin and being *renewed*. He has been thrown out of the old sin-center so as to be placed in a new milieu, the milieu of the original creation and the purpose that the Creator connected

with it. This process is combined with a new *knowledge*;
the Yes leads toward it. It is not merely a result of fleeing
from evil; it does start with the No—"I will not sin any
more!"—but it goes beyond it; "I will do good!" The
No brings forth from itself the Yes. It is not possible for
someone to have cast off the old man and now not know
what to do next; for him in that state to feel forsaken by
everything, even by God; he forsakes the old self in order
to be accepted anew by God, with new stipulations that
are implicit in that knowledge, in the evident fact that
a real process has been completed, in the affirmation of
God's ways. And even though this new life may break in
with cataclysmic force, nevertheless it is made safe immediately, because it is situated in God and it shows from
God's perspective what was left behind in a new light that
makes it comprehensible, so that the new man in faith is
immunized against sin: he realizes what he has been and
detests it.

The first creation was in a temporal sequence: the day
when God created man was preceded by other days of creation. In putting on the new man, there is no gradation
or succession; he comes to be in the coming away from
the old. The No proceeds without development into the
Yes. And knowledge finds its milieu in the word of God
that Christ brought to mankind; this milieu has nothing
to do with the old Tree of Knowledge in the middle of
paradise. Rather, it is found in God and pertains to what
God the Father does through his Son for the redemption
of mankind.

3:11. Here there cannot be Greek and Jew, circumcised and un-circumcised, barbarian, Scythian, slave, free man, but Christ is all, and in all.

All the distinctions that people make as to religion, ethnic origin, social class, are listed here in a quick overview; but only to be erased, only to deprive the usual concepts, which are as familiar to Paul as they are to his listeners, of their lines of demarcation—so that the question spontaneously arises: Now what? Even if one was accustomed to regarding men as Gentiles or Jews, as circumcised or uncircumcised, as slaves or freemen, as natives or barbarians, and was able to pin them down with one of these categories, nevertheless the former sinner, who has become a new man, belongs to none of these categories anymore; he moves about on a plane where these accidental traits are meaningless, where he is not even considered as the new man, *but* as *Christ*. He is recognizable *in all*; his imprint makes them what they are. He determines all the categories. Where merely human, inadequate and sinful qualities prevailed, now the heavenly life of the triune God has revealed and communicated itself. As opposed to the movement spoken of before, from No to Yes, as opposed to this flight from sin and toward God, which appeared as a human activity, a stripping off and a putting on, now only Christ remains visible. The whole meaning of conversion, the whole meaning of the divine image in man rests in him. Man is in the process of becoming; Christ, however, is. So much *is* he, that he *is all and in all*, so that no one can deny his presence within. He is not "here, but not there", does not prefer this place while avoiding that one, does not incline to one and flee another; he is everywhere and in everyone. This is the image of redemption brought to completion, indeed, the image of eternity in heaven, which has taken up all the places and times on earth into itself. And this is no longer the first creation with its localized paradise and one single man within it; this is the entire world with all its inhabitants, gathered in Christ. He is Place; he is Time, in that he is the time of each individual and has pitched his tent, taken up his abode in each one. If one were to ask about the meaning of such omnipresence and about the meaning of human life therein, the answer could come only in him, in his teaching and his relation to the Father and to the Spirit.

3:12. *Put on then, as God's chosen ones, holy and beloved, compassion, kindness, lowliness, meekness, and patience.*

Here everything is led back to the highest center: the Father. He dispenses all graces and awaits every response to them. He chooses them, and on the basis of this generous gift believers bear his mark, which makes them at once *holy* and *beloved*, because in them the Father can see Christ's brethren, clothed with his holiness, beloved for the sake of his love. The Father has not chosen them so as to leave them standing there; they have received with their election a dowry that distinguishes them as being for God. But now they must try to correspond with this gift: to be clothed with the things that God loves, to show that they know about their election, that they are willing to answer the question they pose to everyone [by the very distinction they enjoy]. The answer lies in the qualities they acquire, not by presumption, but because God wishes to find them in his own.

First *compassion*, which pours forth from within them and is one with them and which is their response to God's merciful election. Then come *kindness* and *lowliness*: kindness, so as to love the way God loves; lowliness, because they acknowledge that their love is only on loan from the love of God. *Meekness* they should have like the Lamb of God and *patience*, just as God was long-suffering with them, his ultimate forbearance being that he allowed his Son to become man in order to carry the sins of the world as a Lamb even unto death. God's long-suffering was manifested not only to the sinner but also to the Son in his life and death; to the Son's endurance corresponds an attribute of the Father, by which he endures the redemptive way of the Son even into the abandonment of death. And even though the Father alone knows the hour and to that extent is the One who takes action, still what he does corresponds exactly to the action, to the patience and long-suffering of the Son. All of these attributes, which the Colossians ought to make their own, have meaning as long as they are not torn away from the unity that is formed by election and faith and which rests in the Son. Since the Father created man in his image and likeness, the latter must now try, as a new man, to offer the Father a likeness of the Son, so that the Father can observe both in the union of the Son.

3:13. Forbearing one another and, if one has a complaint against another, forgiving each other; as the Lord has forgiven you, so you also must forgive.

Mutual forbearance is not a dull putting up with someone, nor is it setting a limit to which the other may go and one shall be willing to tolerate him. It is something perfectly positive: a deed at once of insight as well as of patience; because each one should see himself in his neighbor: his own weaknesses and bad habits confront him, while he ought to allow the brother his virtues and strengths and should not forget them when faults are evident. In forbearance lies the recognition of what is good, with the will to forgive what is not. The Christian should take the complaints that he might be justified in expressing and subsume them immediately in an attitude of forgiveness. How much has been forgiven *him*! And if the Father bears the Son's sacrifice on the Cross, then it means that he bears together with the Son all the sins the Son carries as a burden and that he extends on principle the blessing of his forgiveness to all. The Father cannot forgive the Son any sin, since he has committed none; but he can include fully within his forgiveness the sins that the Son bears, because all have been marked with the sign of the Cross. When the Father meets the sinner in the Old Covenant, he does so in righteousness; in the New Covenant he always meets the Son first, the Beloved, to whom he offers in love the infinite sum of his capacity for forgiveness as a response to the sum total of the Son's sacrifice.

When the Father forgives, then Christ *the Lord has for-*

given you. His saying, ''No one comes to the Father except through me'' means this also: that in the Son's forgiveness the Father's forgiveness is obtained. The Son knows that he may dispose freely of everything the Father is willing to grant to mankind; therefore on the Cross he does two things: he forgives his enemies, and he asks the Father to forgive them. He brings the latter forgiveness down from heaven by the fact that he himself forgives and has forgiven on earth. By constantly forgiving all of the mean and ugly things that people do to him, he asks the Father to forgive them also. And hanging on the Cross he is already so near death that he pronounces the request out-right, as if he were already finished, as though he himself did not matter anymore; the Father may reckon him, as he is dying, to be so utterly among men that through him (who is no longer mentioned as an individual) the Father forgives all mankind. To this redemption of mankind he can only give his last blessing: his forgiveness.

3:14. *And above all these put on love, which binds everything together in perfect harmony.*

Paul has enumerated various virtues that are indispensable for believers. But he sees something farther beyond, even greater and more important than these indispensable things. That is *love.* They must put it on like a garment from which they may nevermore be separated, because it is the *binding* force, the chain of *perfection* that draws perfection after it and is one with perfection. The Colossians are acquainted with the virtues Paul has mentioned; they have seen them embodied in the Son and have also encountered them among themselves. For each one they were able to point to this or that person in the community who possesses it; then they notice also how desirable, how indispensable it is. Yet all that should pale now, because love steps forward, bound together with perfection. The Lord alone is perfect, though. Still, his perfection radiates love and grants it to others, so that believers, through the love of the Son, are drawn into his perfection. Here the thought of the Eucharist is quite near. Paul admonishes them to love; therefore they can reach out for love, it is offered to them, they know where it can be obtained. The Lord has bequeathed to them his body and his blood as a sign and a vessel of his love. Human beings, even believers, are weak; they grow tired, slacken their efforts, lose sight of the way, do not even see the love that is offered to them. If they know, then, that they can always reach out for love, the way one reaches for bread and wine, they will realize anew the value of the sacrament, for now love is no longer dependent merely on what they do and what they leave undone. Love comes from the Lord and works within them, and what it brings about is perfection.

Faith and following Christ and all virtues resemble a chain in which the one link draws the other after it, and yet love, which is the highest, the one that brings to completion, is not the last link; in the case of love, one cannot wait until the end; one has to start with it, at every moment it is the next link, because it brings about the unity and the sequence of all the links and is already drawing after itself, with the chain, perfection too as the sum of all virtues, within which those who believe and those who love should strive. In the totality that is offered, all piecework becomes meaningful. Paul has often admonished the Christians not to slacken their efforts, to search for new ways, to strive for new virtues. But the present verse says even more: one thing is sufficient that all may be fulfilled; and the "all" that is fulfilled lies in the one. The one is love; the all is perfection.

A new light falls now on the commandment to love one's neighbor. It is no longer that love that is achieved by an individual and affects another individual. Love rather moves as a link within a chain that signifies perfection. Perfection, though, is always the totality, and the totality always has yet other aspects than those that the person who loves can make visible. And so the person who loves actually offers more than he has, and the person who is embraced by love becomes acquainted with the totality through the bond of perfection. In this way the communion of saints is realized, in that those who love are linked to each other by love and in being so bound also receive their place in the Church.

3:15. *And let the peace of Christ rule in your hearts, to which indeed you were called in the one body. And be thankful.*

Peace binds one member to the other. The virtues are linked to one another by love, and love itself is the most important link in the chain, on which all the others depend. Peace, however, is like the material that makes the linkage possible. It is the distinguishing mark showing that something belongs to the chain. It is found in each individual virtue, in every step toward virtue, in every prayer, every decision in life; even where the heart is obliged to be uneasy, where it hesitates, where difficulties pile up, it still in each case leaves the imprint of sincerity. For it proceeds from the Lord, and it is his peace, which is superior to any peace that an individual might make. It has nothing to do with lukewarmness, with complacency, because it, above all things, characterizes the attitude toward the Father that the Son had, who went forth in the peace of the Father in order to fulfill his mission, who in the peace of the Father walked along the way of the Cross, died at peace with him and through peace rose again. Peace clothes the mission of the Son. And precisely this peace should live *in* the *hearts* of believers, because they walk their way within the mission of the Son. If the Lord were not to dwell in their hearts, they still could strive to attain individual virtues and accomplish individual outstanding deeds, and something could be said for that, but it would all remain the expression of personal effort. If the Lord dwells within them, then even their smallest actions bear the mark of his peace, the stamp of his mission. They belong to him, and he does not deny them.

For believers, peace belongs to God's call. To that peace, they *were called in the one body*, the body of Christ, who came in order to bring us *his* peace, which surpasses every previous concept of peace because it is heavenly, because it consists of a mission, because it means doing battle and because it draws all things into his way, together with the task that he has taken on for love of the Father. That means, therefore, that the believer has to look to the body, to the Incarnation, to the Sacrament of the Body and Blood in order to understand his calling; furthermore that the Christian mission is not an abstract subject; the Christian calling on earth, on the contrary, means the body's battle with all kinds of adversity. The Christian stands, so to speak, with one foot in nature and the other in the supernatural and is not permitted to neglect either for the sake of the other. And in both realms the body of Christ is there before his eyes as an example and a guide, for in both he fulfills the divine mission. And so peace is not only a final link in the sequence; it is essential that it *rule*. It has therefore a prominent place. It ought to arrange all the things God has foreseen and keep them in order, so that the central place, the Lord's mission, will remain available in each person who is called.

And when the Christian regards his mission in its natural relationship to the things of this world, then he is not allowed to sigh, or to measure his weakness against the excessive burden of the task, or to go over his failures, or succumb to fear, but now is the time to *be thankful*. Thankful the way a Christian is after Communion, when he has received the Body of Christ, for he is allowed to remember also that the Lord not only took on a body, but he also gave one to him, so that he might make use of it in his mission and might possess in it a weapon with which to battle for Christian peace. It becomes apparent here that everything has its ultimate permanence in the body of the Lord, and for precisely this reason thanksgiving is the ultimate way a person who is called can testify to his God that he exists. When someone speculates in lofty terms about Christian charity and then looks at what he has actually accomplished, he has to lose heart. When he looks, though, from his own body to the body of Christ, who did the will of God completely, and considers at the same time that this body is given to him in the Blessed Sacrament, he is so thoroughly outdone that nothing remains for him but thankfulness.

3:16. *Let the word of Christ dwell in you richly, as you teach and admonish one another in all wisdom, and as you sing psalms and hymns and spiritual songs with thankfulness in your hearts to God.*

The *word of Christ* is identical with him, yet it is at the same time his entire teaching; so it is both: vessel and content, love and knowledge. And this word should *dwell* abundantly. Believers therefore should open their hearts to it without restraint, they should exert all their abilities in order to grasp it, reserve for it so much room within themselves that it can expand there, genuinely dwelling in and occupying the rooms that are offered, making use of and alterations to them as it pleases. There is always the idea of duration connected with dwelling, an adaptation that transforms, a taking possession according to one's own customs. Paul would not want to hear that the Colossians have only a small, temporary place left over for the word. The room should be *rich* and should allow for extensions.

And the Apostle instructs them about how they should show hospitality to the word: with *psalms and hymns and spiritual songs*, with *thanksgiving* but also *in grace*, in joy that they are permitted to receive the word as their guest. This joy is not mute but rather breaks into song and is closely connected with the word, giving it expression and more room to live in, deepening knowledge, involving the things of the Old Covenant, the promises and their fulfillment by the Lord and the Church, and presenting all of it in the form of song *to God*. Furthermore the singer presents himself, too, and grows in his insight into the word. Through chanting, the words of the Psalms awaken him to new life; he understands what they mean; he rejoices because of them and with them. Song is the expression of joy; joy in God's presence is always grateful, a response to his grace. It is also a useful joy that *teaches . . . in all wisdom*—whereby each member of the community ought to communicate to the other what he knows —and simultaneously *admonishes*, so that each one helps the other on the way to God. This song is liturgy but at the same time humanly helpful; the life of the young community is fostered, protected, strengthened; it is ecclesiastical care but also ecclesiastical instruction for the individual and for all. And song is the thanksgiving that looks back on everything and pulls everything together, that always leaves room for new *spiritual songs*, which are granted to individuals in grace, or to the community in the same grace. The mere sentiment of gratitude is not enough for Paul; thanks should take a tangible form, and the word of God itself makes plenty of patterns available. This joyful utterance is the expression of the Church's love, the communion of saints. Sacred song is a community action, even when individuals express themselves therein; it is liturgical, with tradition already built into it, whether it is Christian singing or the Old Testament hymns of praise.

3:17. *And whatever you do, in word or deed, do everything in the name of the Lord Jesus, giving thanks to God the Father through him.*

Thanksgiving to God is to be found not only in song, instruction and admonition but also in every *word* and in every *deed*. The Christian cannot distance himself from any one of his utterances; everything in his life should reveal that he is a Christian. What he says or does must witness to his awareness that God is present: God the Son, God the Father, who can be reached through the Son. The *name of the Lord* is the living seed, which sprouts in works or words; in his name believers live, so that when the Lord dwells in them, they announce his indwelling by their entire existence. Being is part of serving; it follows that they do not set about serving Christ only at specified hours, while reserving others for themselves and for the world, and the last hours of their life perhaps for God; they exist plainly and simply in the name of the Lord. In this name they live their life. And so their *giving thanks*, too, has the same dimensions as their existence; they have to give thanks in everything because thanking is part of doing and the witness of a Christian life is part of living. And they thank *God the Father* through the Lord; their thanksgiving is acquainted with the mystery of the Three in One. Therefore it is demanded of them that they be one, which in itself gives witness to God's living unity and to the integral life of the person who gives thanks, who lives for the Lord and who through him receives a share in the unity of God. This way of unity is found in thanksgiving. Thanking is a form of love and thus knows no exclusion. One cannot be grateful for certain things in his life and exclude other things; nor can one thank one Divine Person and skip over the others. As we give thanks, the knowledge of God's own unity and an awareness of his working in us are brought again to mind and impressed upon our memory. And if thanksgiving-as-love knows no exclusion, then in thanking we are so close to God that we receive anew from him the love that makes our Christian life possible. We give thanks in unity, but in this unity we learn anew what the Father intends for us, what the Son has granted us with redemption and what the Spirit communicates to us in animating our faith and in blowing through the Church.

3:18. *Wives, be subject to your husbands, as is fitting in the Lord.*

A sentence that one cannot divide in two, the first half of which leads immediately to the second. Wives, then, have their proper place in the great order that the Lord brings. Even if his teaching is dissected into ever so many individual precepts and brings countless mysteries to light and hints at others that for the moment cannot be aired, it remains always a teaching of order, which consists from all eternity in the trinitarian life and which the Son on earth reflects in his Church. It is not a matter here of order for the sake of order, but rather it is in the work of redemption the assimilation of earth to heaven—in the Church, which binds the two together. Wives, by their subordination to their husbands, are fit into a hierarchical order. Each married woman should be subject to her husband, but subordination is itself an expression of ecclesiastical life; it is determined by faith and is aware that it is from the Lord. It underlines the order in creation. God had created Adam and Eve one after the other and also one beside the other. Sin destroyed the complementary equality that God willed for marriage, the naturally supernatural character and the supernaturally natural quality of the relationship between husband and wife. The husband was placed as master over the wife, who is to bring forth children in pain. In the Lord, marriage is instituted anew. A certain subordination in love remains, but it is accompanied by a blessing. The Son is constantly subject to the will of the Father; as Son, as God, he does the will of the Father, but he does it also as man, so comprehensively, in fact, that men in their relationships are able to live by his accomplishment. Subordination now is no longer coercion or distressing humiliation; it is sanctification that leads to the Lord, an ordering into his order. A wife, however, is sustained not simply by her Lord but also by her husband, whom Paul next admonishes.

3:19. *Husbands, love your wives, and do not be harsh with them.*

This love, then, is the answer to subordination. But subordination also has to be the answer to the love of husbands. Because the former belongs to the Lord, so too the husband's love for his wife belongs to him. If any love belongs to him, though, then it is sanctified and derives from the Lord's love for mankind. *Do not be harsh with them*: this commandment, too, reciprocates the wife's

subordination: what is sinful and domineering has to van-
ish from the husband's side of the relationship. If God is
love, then love appears as all-encompassing and belongs to
every manner of being and manifestation of God. Love,
which in God is undivided life, is granted to men in such
a way that they find in it the answer to their questions, and
also to the questions they pose to one another by their
coexistence and co-belonging. And other than in love,
these questions are insoluble. The commandment of subordination and the prohibition of harshness are both ongoing lessons in love. Love in marriage is not that charm
surrounding inexperience that is attractive at the start and
that allegedly does not last afterward; love is so completely
grounded in the word of God that comes from God that
it endures beyond all human relationships. And the ordering of marriage is the order of love. Since children,
too, belong to this order, they must fit into it as well; as
soon as they can understand what is said, they must put
up with an admonishment from the Apostle.

3:20. *Children, obey your parents in everything, for this pleases
the Lord.*

The children, too, have to obey, not for obedience' sake,
but for *the Lord*, whom this *pleases*. And if they are supposed to practice obedience *in everything*, even in matters they do not understand, then it is because it makes
sense in the Lord. This holding-in-trust of understanding,
which was established in the Lord, is good for children
as well. Even grown-up believers, when they accept an
admonition, receive instruction or pray, can run into a

zone of mystery where understanding leaves off. There they are like children. But children have a special claim to what is mysterious about God, to that revelation of the mystery of love that is expressed in the words: *for this pleases the Lord.* That is the answer to all questions that children can ask, and with increasing age they will understand better what kind of a place this acceptable way is, and they will manage to stay in it. But for the moment it is a sufficient answer, which also makes the Lord's love visible to children and relates it to childlike obedience. The Church's ordinances lead to God's order, and part of this is that children should experience what is acceptable to God. The grown-up understands to some extent why he must do this or that in order to fulfill God's will. To be sure, there are mysteries hiding everywhere, but that does not make him uneasy, because he has points of reference by which he can tell whether his life is orderly and righteous. The child does not yet understand that much; therefore there is more room for authority. But when he is told that this way it is acceptable to the Lord, then the unadorned statement, "That's how it is" puts on a friendly face.

The subordination of wives, the avoidance of harshness by husbands, the obedience of children: all belong to the same Church, all are an expression of the same teaching, the same love for great and small. Heaven bends down over the earth for all of them in the same way. Understanding can come by degrees, but love can be the same at every stage and in all its forms.

3:21. *Fathers, do not provoke your children, lest they become discouraged.*

The believer needs encouragement, for the way he travels is one of growing responsibilities and difficulties. He cannot walk it if he is spiritually impoverished and dry. He requires cheering up and also a certain measure of success, certain kinds of relief, at least at the start. And especially children (who are similar to those who stand at the beginning of their faith journey) need encouragement. God grants it to believers in the form of consolations, in the sense that they are broadening their knowledge of him. Therefore *fathers* also should *not provoke* their *children*, should not show any harshness toward them. In the same way they pattern their relationship to their spouse upon the love of the Lord, so too their instructions to their children. They should be so firmly rooted in the Church that they can draw upon her experiences and customs to show their children the way. The consequences of losing heart are not described; only the prohibition is laid down. It is as though Paul were here forbidding anyone ever to use toward children the full measure of severity that he himself applies on occasion with evildoers. And just as he again and again happens upon mysteries in the Lord that do not belong to our time-bound existence and whose disclosure does not seem urgent, so he does not feel obliged in his instructions to give reasons for everything. Nevertheless, points of comparison present themselves everywhere between children and catechumens, between those who are entering more fully into life and those who are entering more fully into the Church; both journeys require courage, and the fathers bear the responsibility. Such responsibility of love, which becomes visible in family life, is not limited to this, because it is an ecclesiastical responsibility that lives in the Lord and has its expression in him. And so from the children and the fathers, Paul goes farther, beyond the framework of the immediate family and on to slaves, who belong to the family in an extended sense and likewise have their place in the Church's order.

3:22. *Slaves, obey in everything those who are your earthly masters, not with eyeservice, as men-pleasers, but in singleness of heart, fearing the Lord.*

Paul makes the same demand of slaves as he does of children: to *obey in everything*. They have with respect to the family a standing similar to that of children: they are not burdened with the full responsibility of parents, and yet the domestic structure binds and regulates and obligates them in a particular way. They obey their *masters*. They are *earthly*, which gives them a symbolic role. Toward the children their role is not symbolic; then they are real parents, obliged by a natural responsibility to raise their children. Toward slaves, however, they only take the place of the true master, the Lord. So that the slave possesses in his master something analogous to what believers have in one of the saints of the Church: an intercessor, who communicates to him the commands of the Lord so clearly that he can walk the way of obedience easily. Just as the saint seems to carry within himself the entire teaching of Christ and yet again and again illustrates an individual aspect of it, so too masters take on with respect to slaves an intercessory office on behalf of the Lord. By virtue of their position, they have the right to demand obedience; they are masters according to the flesh because behind them stands One who is so according to the spirit and who demands obedience from both masters and slaves.

Because the masters are a symbol, slaves must obey, *not with eyeservice*, not merely for the sake of human respect, not only when the master is watching, but constantly. There is no such thing as a hierarchical power that can be disengaged at certain times, just as there is no discipleship for limited hours only. The constancy of earthly service has its pattern in the constancy of following the Lord. But the symbol is there in order to yield at the proper time to the genuine Master. For obedience does not consist in being *men-pleasers*, in amusing the masters, but in being enlisted in the service of the Lord, under the watchful eye of the Father, who sees everything. The earthly master steps back, then, behind his prototype. He does not on that account have to ease off, for the Lord is indeed present when the earthly master commands, and because the obedience that is shown to the latter is considered to be in reality rendered to the Lord. This parable-in-action makes compliance easier; it offers assistance, as "the acceptable way in the Lord" does with the obedience of children. When difficulties arise and the slaves do not know how they should act, then may they keep this parallel between the master and the Lord before their eyes, so as to find the proper order of obedience. They obey in time but unto eternity.

Their obedience should be *in singleness of heart*, so plain and simple that it wastes no time on second thoughts and objections. It does not watch for the master's mistakes so as to make excuses for itself, because obedience is a good thing and because everything belongs to the Lord and to his Church. *Fearing the Lord.* Slaves recognize the presence of the Lord, and they fear nothing more than doing something that displeases the Lord. There is a kind of shelter and security in this obedience, which also bestows certainty, the hallmark of the right path.

Within all this order the Lord appears at various places, under various forms. Where marriage is concerned, he is more the Lord of order; with children, more the Lord of love. With regard to slaves, fear is mentioned. But each quality is from the Lord and is, moreover, perfect, and each one completes the others and belongs to them. Just as in human society everything has its counterpart: husband and wife, father and child, master and slave, so too Paul shows the complementarity in the Lord himself. Therefore nothing in the Church is peripheral; one thing always completes the other in such a way that the Lord's greatness and love appear visibly, together with everything he accomplishes for mankind in union with the Father and the Spirit; consequently everyone, whatever his station in life may be or the degree of his progress in the faith or his hesitancy or his zeal, experiences the need to go on farther, because the one thing necessary finds its fulfillment in the Lord alone. The Lord, though, is not one thing for one person and something else for another; in his unique Otherness, he is, as Paul shows, always the selfsame Eternal One, who demands one faith and who governs the Church. And so the various complementary positions of men with regard to one another are also parables for their various positions with respect to the Church, which they have to serve, too, and in which they must occupy their place in order to be in good standing with the Lord.

3:23. *Whatever your task, work heartily, as serving the Lord and not men.*

All the slave's chores are combined in the one service rendered to the Lord; thus they are elevated above everyday routine and filled with a new significance that remains mysterious, because it comes into immediate contact with what belongs to the Lord. The slave should work *as serving the Lord*; and it might be difficult for him at first to understand how the small, trifling, almost useless or repugnant things he does can be the Lord's property. But Paul says it with the authority of his office; it already has, therefore, an official importance for *him*, but he does not speak for himself, but for the Lord's sake. He is only a middleman, and when he steps back and only his word remains, then the slave sees the connection between his inconspicuous efforts and God, who accepts them. Then he no longer needs to regard his work as a "sacrifice" that is offered with a sigh or with constant calculations but instead as a deed done *heartily*, wholeheartedly, in faith and love. To do something gladly does not necessarily mean to do it without effort but, rather, without grumbling and with the awareness of giving a gift thereby. Slaves do not have to be impressed by the exalted character of this gift; they need only to be filled with love for the Lord. Indeed, they will love the Lord that much more when he deigns to confer importance upon what is unimportant because he loves what they are doing.

And not men. Men are prone to underestimate and disdain the work of others. They do not want to do it themselves, and so they act as though it were unimportant. It is not easy to work for ill-tempered people; how much more beautiful, then, it is to work for the Lord, who offers in return all that he has. This *and not men* is, at first glance, a peculiar interpretation of the Lord's commandment: "Love your neighbor!" But Paul makes it comprehensible by adding: *serving the Lord.* The neighbor is to be loved in the Lord; human work is to be accomplished within the framework of the divine requirement; sacrifices are to be made in a spirit of joyful self-giving; hence slaves appear no longer to be a particularly oppressed or inferior class of men but persons who share in the wishes of the Lord and who were chosen to fulfill them. And if they know this, they gladly do everything *heartily.*

3:24. *Knowing that from the Lord you will receive the inheritance as your reward; you are serving the Lord Christ.*

All of the slaves' work is done with the knowledge that there is an *inheritance.* Therefore they are related to the Lord directly, shareholders in what he inherits. And this as a *reward*, as payment. The picture of the Lord being drawn here is especially attractive for those who serve: he came in the name of the Father and of the Spirit and became, in the society of men, a man who serves, in such a way, though, that he did not distance himself thereby in the least from the Father or from heaven. As man he performed manual labor and later did the work of the Kingdom of God, in order finally to haul the burden of sin and to die under it. Yet precisely this work that he accomplishes brings about the Kingdom, indeed it is the Kingdom; in laboring he bestows it, he divides his inheritance; he distributes it in the gift of faith and for the faith. The inheritance is the reward for faith. Therefore it is not true that man on earth accomplishes a sheerly secular task and God in turn pays out to him in heaven eternal life as a heavenly wage. The share in the inheritance lies more in the faith and in the love that God grants to mankind and that men and women then apply in human measure to the work for the Kingdom of God, to the service of the Lord. Just as the Son laboring on earth *is* the Kingdom of Heaven distributing itself, so also the Kingdom of Heaven becomes the inheritance of those charitable believers who, in faith and love, are laboring together with the Son. The faith the Lord bestows on us is so strong that it makes us rightful heirs. The love of the Lord is so powerful that it overcomes our weakness, and heaven is then the wage for those who believe and love on earth. But this wage is no longer something commensurate with a human accomplishment; God shows thereby that his love is not at all scandalized by the pettiness of human love, that he fills faith with so much of his might that our powerlessness ceases to matter, that our accomplishment gains a share in his, our human existence takes part in his divine life. The reward is not made according to any measure; it can be compared with absolution, which in an incomprehensible way eradicates the entire sin. The reward shows none of the marks of what it appears to repay: there is no trace of petty, calculating, hesitant human deeds. The reward is perfect.

You are serving the Lord Christ. With this Paul invites his listeners to a totality; what he has explained previously should now be realized. The slave is no longer the vassal of some lord or other; he has Christ the Lord to serve. He is that much more intimately bound to the Lord. His human service belongs, just like the service of any other Christian, to the Lord; like anyone, he has to put his earthly life in the service of eternal life. Before, Paul was indicating particular paths; now it is a matter of doing the whole thing. Everyone who works can keep this word constantly before his eyes; everything troublesome about his work will be absorbed into it. Disappointments, setbacks do not prevent him from knowing that he stands in exactly the same place where Paul, where the first apostles stood: in the place that God himself has assigned to him.

3:25. *For the wrongdoer will be paid back for the wrong he has done, and there is no partiality.*

In faith there is a repayment for what one has done in living faith and in charity, and this reward surpasses anything that can be imagined. But there is also—and no one is exempt, be he master or slave—punishment, which is meted out according to a man's deeds, "with no respect of persons", that is, without *partiality*. God alone sees the heart. God sees *wrongdoing*, the lack of faith or of love for him and for his work. And judgment is pronounced accordingly. Slaves were exalted by Paul: they had the privilege of serving the Lord directly; they could move up to the places reserved for his chosen coworkers. But for a Christian there is no haughtiness in holding a special place. There is no respect of persons, only love, which demands love in return: divine love that wants human love, the gift of faith that awaits the act of faith. Everything apart from that, every unjust deed will *be paid back for the wrong* that has been *done.* In no way are slaves now in a position that allows them more leeway than others, that could place them any higher in heaven simply because they were less privileged on earth; the Lord, as man, was indistinguishably one of us, not conspicuous for being either above or below us. And through his Incarnation the brotherhood of mankind has been restored, and among brothers no respect of persons can prevail. Nevertheless the Father will favor the one who wants to do his will together with the Son, and the Son will favor the one who has accepted the entire gift of faith and allows it to bear fruit in each of his acts of service.

4:1. *Masters, treat your slaves justly and fairly, knowing that you also have a Master in heaven.*

Masters should give what is *just and fair*, and to do that they must appreciate what the services are worth; they should develop their relationship with their slaves on the foundation of justice. This human relationship, however, is hemmed in on all sides by an eternal one. And so they should not devise a merely human justice, in which all-too-human errors will be inherent; neither should they take their personal good will as the standard for determining what is just and fair, but rather keep on *knowing that you also have a Master in heaven*, who will treat them as they have treated their slaves. The social gradations that form a part of human life have no validity before God, and masters must acknowledge that their Lord is over them at the distance that separates God from mankind. A distance that is infinitely more serious and final than the minute secular distance between a lord and his vassal, because he has all of eternity at his disposal. To that extent masters have it harder than slaves. The latter carry out their tasks and strive to shape them into a service rendered to the Lord. Masters, though, in a certain sense must themselves show forth the image of God; they must become well versed in the standard of his justice, so as to allot to their slaves what is just, even as God will do to them in turn. It is precisely in this that the office of masters is more time-bound, too, than the office of slaves; they will have to separate themselves from it, and ultimately it will cease to exist, because the office of master belongs in eternity to God alone. In their short time on earth, however, masters should practice justice toward their slaves, so as to learn how to stand before God's justice. Their death will be a rupture, as far as their office is concerned, . . . but then again no interruption, because faith and love endure and because God himself assigned to masters their place on earth and now expects from them the fruits of it. In faith he showed them the qualities that they in particular were required to cultivate. Finally: they were, as masters, vassals, who received their office on loan from God in order to render it to him again in the way that the one Lord and Master wills: together with the fruits of faith and with the deeds of charity, which for them ought to be acts of justice.

EXHORTATIONS AND GREETINGS

4:2. Continue steadfastly in prayer, being watchful in it with thanksgiving.

The ordering of the various stations in life repeatedly juxtaposed the Lord in heaven and the Church on earth; heaven seemed to be there for the earth and the earth for heaven. But the word, conversation was still missing. The sole connection seemed to be human conduct, which had to be careful about heaven so as to be proper. But now prayer breaks forth, the word that represents the key to heaven, as the essential thing that should be fostered *steadfastly*. They should treat prayer like a jewel, *being watchful in it*, indeed, with *thanksgiving*. They should apply themselves to it totally, with their whole soul. Paul says it in sober terms; his exhortation to prayer stands beside many others. And yet the believers must hear it as a most important point. Prayer is not something yet to be added on, still waiting in some corner or other to be taken into consideration; it is something that demands the entire vigilant attention of their mind, so that those who pray must keep watch over their own vigilance in order to be equal to the task, must overcome their weariness, their inclination to be busy with other things, and their lukewarmness so as to be awake and at the same time watchful and to pray with the full force of their mind and of their faith. And they should not feel that prayer is merely one duty among others but that it is a gift, for which they have to give thanks. They should give thanks, not only that their toilsome life may find a lasting and blessed reward in heaven, but also for the fact that they are permitted to pray on earth, that God hears what they say, that a possibility exists for this constant conversation. Even though only two of its characteristics, watchfulness and thanksgiving, are evident for the time being, prayer in fact produces the durable bond between Creator and creature, the Christian and the Lord, the working person and the Holy Spirit. To the work of prayer, however, belongs thanksgiving as well, which should be rendered spontaneously and with love: for the fact that one may pray at all, that God inclines his ear, that he allows man to stand before him as a speaker. Viewed thus, being watchful and attentive in prayer is no longer wearisome but refreshing, because it finally provides an opportunity to express thanksgiving, because finally man can tell God how grateful he is to him, that in his presence he may ponder the gift of God, so as to become conscious of it in love.

4:3. *And pray for us also, that God may open to us a door for the word, to declare the mystery of Christ, on account of which I am in prison.*

In the prayer of gratitude there is room for personal concerns and petitions. In prayer, which is an ongoing accompaniment to the Christian life, there is room for orderliness. It will not be lost. This is not to say that there can ever be enough of giving thanks, but in thanksgiving and in watchfulness all kinds of things can be thought of which are of the Lord; and the Apostle, who is exhorting those who pray, can claim a place for himself here. He is not here as someone from outside who is keeping tabs on the progress of his brethren, whether they are following his ordinances and taking his exhortations to heart; he stands among them as one of them, who is called together with them and works together with them. Only his task is a special one: the *word*. The service of the word. What he needs most urgently is that the word be heard, that he find the right expression for it. That it be understood not only in a human way but in the divine fullness that makes up its content. So they should pray *that God may open to us a door for the word* to be proclaimed: that God will open a door for himself! That God will fashion Paul as his instrument in such a way that it will be suited to the work. The word that Paul proclaims is the word of the Lord; he must proclaim it as God wills, but in order that his will be done it needs human intercession. An entire life cycle of prayer becomes evident here, for the dispenser of the word is himself dependent upon the word; the one who exhorts needs support and reinforcement in order to *declare the mystery of Christ*. This mystery, which is the mystery of the triune God, is rolled up together in the word and remains there a mystery for every believer, even for Paul. It is the Lord's property, mysterious property, that flows like an ever-broadening stream into heaven, to the place to which no man has ever penetrated: to the vision of the Father.

On account of which I am in prison. On account of his witness, on account of the Lord himself, Paul lies in chains. He is therefore at the place the word has allowed him to reach. Yet even this incarceration, even his will and impulse to find an opening for the word, do not unveil for him the depths of the mystery that is to be proclaimed. He is moved by it, he was converted by it; now it has put him into chains, and in the course of his life he has understood much about it; but when he speaks about love or faith or hope, he knows only as much about it as a believing, loving, hoping man can, whereas the fullness of the word remains in the Lord. He receives lights that radiate from it, understands certain aspects that point the way through the Lord and beyond into the mystery of the Father; Paul has caught such glimpses and lives by them, without ever actually fathoming their depths. The mystery remains; this is a part of the distance between the Lord, who is the Word, and the man who believes it; between the teaching in its totality and the member that shares in it, between heaven and earth. But there is still the power of prayer, the power of heaven upon which Paul makes a claim, so as to be able to point to it and to lead others into the truth of the Lord. He is so totally an apostle and a believer that he has been drawn completely into this spiritual circulation—as every believer ultimately ought to be—from heaven to earth and back again to heaven, and he finds in prayer his daily sustenance, and in worship his strength.

4:4. *That I may make it clear, as I ought to speak.*

When the Son reveals on earth the fullness of the triune life, he does so without restriction, since the entire fullness dwells in him in bodily form. He, for his part, sets no boundaries for his proclamation; he does not conceal the fact that what is shown passes over into boundless mystery, because men, on account of their distance, will understand at any moment only a part of what is revealed. Speech and silence are one and the same in the Son, because God the Father hears the whole word, of course, while men and women hear only as much as is possible for them, humanly and in faith.

Now, though, Paul has the commission to *speak* of this word. That is, not just to speak in general, but *as* he ought, according to his mission, a predetermined plan that is to be followed, in which his understanding and his proclamation fuse into a unity. He must say everything he knows and unveil the mystery as far as he can, conscious nevertheless that his proclamation is earthly and remains piecework: a fragment that has its totality in the Lord, in the triune God, in heaven's eternity. He sees, as it were, a small facet of an infinitely large precious stone. When he speaks of God-made-Man, he knows that every description, every word he says about him goes beyond what is seen and experienced and spreads out into the mystery of his divinity. The Son is the gateway to the Father; the Apostle, however, should be the gateway of the word, and since he is a common man among men, his gate is not high, his way is narrow. Still, he has to keep to the duty that God has imposed on him, devote himself to

wholehearted service of the word and submerge himself
in the task, so *that I may make it clear, as I ought to speak*:
in an obedience that he owes to God and that demands
of him the impossible—because it is too much, because
it contains within its mystery the surpassing greatness of
the Lord—an obedience that nevertheless does not try
to adapt this demand to a human format, since a mission
from the Lord cannot assume such limited proportions
but must by its very nature remain divine, overflowing
on every side. Only in this way will Paul not speak his
own word or about his knowledge of the mystery but will
stay within the mysterious truth of God and announce
what is divine and not merely human, proclaim what is
alive in God and is meant to live on in faith. Through
faith he must grope his way again and again toward the
greatness and perfection of God, without ever reaching
it. It is not his human powers that render Paul equal to
the task; it is divine powers, which can be the fruit of
prayer offered on earth. And for this reason the Apostle
needs prayer, not only for himself in order to complete
his task and thereby experience satisfaction, but likewise
for the others who are meant to hear the word through
him.

4:5. *Conduct yourselves wisely toward outsiders; making the
most of the time.*

Both the *conduct* and the *time* belong to Christians in a special way, for the time in which they live is a time of grace
and, to that extent, is derived from the eternal "time" of
God; the power by which they live is heavenly power.

God created time in the beginning; man has misused it: in time he strayed into sin. As a result, time, which was running out and had to end, became a time of increasing sinfulness, a time that by sin had been taken away from God—as though men had really been capable of taking it from God's grasp. And the Son came to make from this passing time of sin a sacred time, to enfold within it his presence, his vision of the Father. So now believers, too, must make out of their time a sacred time and turn their walk into a walk toward holiness. Indeed, now they walk on earth in God's presence, but the community they form does not embrace all men; their faith singles them out. There are nonbelievers besides, who use the passing time in their own way—who observe, though, how Christians use time and notice something of the *wisdom* that is characteristic of them. Thus Christians become a sign for the world.

They should *make the most of* their time, "redeem" it, restore its lost value by re-presenting the sacred time of the Lord in their own time. The outsiders should notice that, too: not only do Christians become different as they walk their walk, but they also transform the present times together with themselves. One of the most important means to obtain this is prayer, wherein the Christian strides beyond his own passing time and manages to let in God's permanence: into his own life, but also into earthly time in general, into the world of the Church and into the world outside the Church. Prayer transforms the relationship to heaven in the sense of faith, a sense, however, that is also included in the vision that the Son has of the Father.

4:6. *Let your speech always be gracious, seasoned with salt, so that you may know how you ought to answer every one.*

If the word was an essential component of Paul's task, so too it is in a similar way for other Christians. Their *speech* is entrusted to them as a duty. They must not present a Church of silence and ignorance; they should be able to speak. To speak a word that leans upon the Word who is the Lord, that is full of his *graciousness* and attractive, a word that is pleasant to hear and that shows faith to be, not the lonely accomplishment of an isolated individual, but a bond with the Divine Word. The word of the believer belongs to the Lord, who is the Word; it is a proclamation from the Lord; in no way has the speaker acquired such a claim to the word that he can dispose of it as he thinks best, that he can imprint upon it the mark of his own personality. He receives the word of grace together with the faith, in one act of God's self-giving to him.

His word should be *seasoned with salt*; it cannot be lukewarm and flat and boring. It should have a character that awakens the interest and curiosity of listeners: speakers and hearers as well should be impressed by the savor of the word. The Christian who speaks, too, through the right use of the word receives seasoned nourishment, which enables him to know how he *ought to answer every one*. Thus the savor of God's word unites speakers and listeners into a community, an incipient Church. The Church comes into being through the word, the gift of the Son-Word to mankind after he fulfilled each of his own words as a deed. The isolation from other people in which the

Christian finds himself upon accepting the word is always burst open by the power of the word itself, so as to bring forth the Church, the community, catholicity.

4:7. *Tychicus will tell you all about my affairs; he is a beloved brother and faithful minister and fellow servant in the Lord.*

In the words with which Paul singles out Tychicus it becomes apparent what Christian love between servants and masters should look like. It is obvious that they, loving the Lord, love one another. This love is a prerequisite for service. When Paul asked earlier for prayers, he did so in the knowledge that his listeners would do it out of love for him; love imposes loving obligations. In the same knowledge he assumes that they like to hear news about him, not so as to have something to talk about, but simply out of Christian love. *Tychicus will tell* them *all about my affairs*, with a truthfulness that stems from the truth of Christian doctrine. This guarantees that his report will be, not gossip, but substance, which can revitalize their Christianity. Many of the things Paul encounters and does are saturated with love and so are apt to awaken new love. But he does not want to say everything himself; instead he leaves material for Tychicus to discuss. As a *fellow servant* the latter is entitled to present matters from his perspective, in his light, which is also a light of love. As a *faithful minister* he receives from God lessons in love, which he then in Christian freedom is authorized to share at his discretion.

4:8. *I have sent him to you for this very purpose, that you may know how we are and that he may encourage your hearts.*

When the Lord promises before his Ascension to *send* the Holy Spirit, then his intentions concern the Church. He wants to strengthen the apostles in their faith and also to communicate to them something of heaven, to make known to them something of his eternal might. Between the promise of the Spirit and the pouring out of the Spirit there is a very exact parallel, which manifests this heavenly might: to individuals as well as to the entire Church. According to the parallel the sending has a precise significance, which in turn is the same meaning to be found in our Lord's sending out his disciples during his life on earth: then, too, it was a matter of communicating signs of his presence, carrying out his mission and at the same time performing works of sanctification. This sending remains meaningful for the Church in the time after the Ascension also. Even in a case where the one sending is no longer explicitly the Lord and the one sent is no longer the Holy Spirit or one of the first apostles.

Paul says that he is *sending* someone for the purpose that *you may know how we are.* He sends a representative, a middleman who is charged with certain tasks but who will also give a report based on his own experience, one who is obedient and insightful at the same time. Among the many members of the Church, each one has the right to know what is going on in the body; solidarity is indispensable to the meaning of the apostolate. Besides, the Colossians are a great distance away: they might feel neglected, abandoned: by Paul or even by God himself, especially if they do not understand the Apostle's imprisonment. The messengers who are sent will clarify the situation for them, explain to them Paul's bond with the Lord, his suffering of what remains yet to be suffered, his role of challenging the world's complacency. That will *encourage* their *hearts*; precisely the plight of the Apostle will serve as a consolation to them and will unite them to him anew in charity. Yes, Paul's sufferings will convey to them a deeper understanding of the Lord's Passion; Paul's proclamation will bring the Lord's word close to them. And praying for Paul will provide them with new openings to heaven. And the human traits that will figure in the report of Tychicus will impress more deeply upon them the human characteristics of the Church, from which the light of heaven shines forth. What happens to her is the will of the Father; to defend the Apostle is to defend Christ's cause, the faith. The news therefore will nourish their prayer, reaffirm their stance and fan the flames of new knowledge and new zeal in their own apostolate. The Apostle's fetters will strengthen their ties with God.

4:9. *And with him Onesimus, the faithful and beloved brother, who is one of yourselves. They will tell you of everything that has taken place here.*

Not by chance is Onesimus described in exactly the same terms as Tychicus: beloved, brother and faithful. It is the expression of loving solidarity. It is the grace of love that makes the brothers appear equally dear and faithful. Through the teaching of Christ, the duties they have taken on and their readiness, they have become equals in the service of the Church. For the Colossians, Onesimus has another special quality: he is *one of yourselves*. One of them and sent to them with the unfamiliar brother; and by the fact that they know him, he offers them a guarantee for *everything that has taken place here*. This is a human consideration that fosters their faith and gives them a sense of involvement. *They will tell you of everything*: both of them, the acquaintance and the stranger, will combine their reports together into one. The Church accepts everyone who professes the faith, but she does not therefore overlook natural bonds and duties; on the contrary, she values them highly wherever this can be for the greater glory of God. As members of the Church, Tychicus and Onesimus are equal; for the Colossians, though, the brother with whom they are acquainted has certain advantages. They know his word, and the word of someone known will lend more weight to that of a stranger, whereas the word of Tychicus will give to that of Onesimus a broader horizon; the Church appears in this: in the fate of the Apostle, which concerns and affects both acquaintances and strangers; in the Christian teaching that unites all, acquaintances and strangers; in sending out her adherents so as to consolidate everywhere the sense of the Church.

4:10. *Aristarchus my fellow prisoner greets you, and Mark the cousin of Barnabas (concerning whom you have received instructions—if he comes to you, receive him)*.

Aristarchus is Paul's *fellow prisoner*: his greeting is, so to speak, an official proof of the solidarity of the suffering, imprisoned Church with the Church that is operating in freedom. To the latter belongs the greeting of *Mark*, who is described as *the cousin of Barnabas*. Whereas the Jews were accustomed to pray to God in one Person, Christians should always see in their prayer to God the life of the Triune. The Son on earth refers constantly to his relation to the Father and to the Spirit and is not to be understood apart from this relation. The Church, too, is a life-connection, in that there are missions or sendings of individual persons. These should not carry out their task in isolation but in connection with the communion of saints, which for the individual is to be found concretely in fellowship with other believers in his walk of life.

The Colossians have already *received instructions* about Mark: When he comes, he should be welcomed. The charitable service that they ought to perform for him is a sort of response to the charitable service that Paul and his companions have rendered to the Colossians. Charity as prayer is indispensable, but by its very nature it carries over into work, not only to make the neighbor's job easier, but also to celebrate the love of the Lord, who continues to perform great works in his Church, through which he keeps alive the faith in the divine life. Therefore every simple word that Paul speaks in his chain is not only a word of faith but also an act of charity for his neighbor, which instructs and admonishes the brethren and brings them closer to the workings of the triune love.

4:11. . . . *and Jesus who is called Justus. These are the only men of the circumcision among my fellow workers for the kingdom of God, and they have been a comfort to me.*

With this new greeting Paul makes the situation of his coworkers visible. Mark and Justus are *of the circumcision*, have come from the Old Covenant to the New; at the same time they are the only ones who are *fellow workers* with Paul *for the kingdom of God*, who by faith evidently have become apostles. They have likewise understood that faith is not a private matter, that the Lord in his gift of himself grants faith as a summons to self-giving and expands the joy of being allowed to believe into a joy of collaborating in the Kingdom of God. For this is how he, the Son, understood the commission he received from the Father. Paul's brothers have become *a comfort* to him. Perhaps from a personal perspective, in that his plight as a prisoner was easier to endure if the believers recognized in it a sign from the Lord. But certainly also from an official perspective, since he sees the seed that he himself has sown sprouting now in the field where the brothers work, in the right way, without slackening off. When Paul asked for prayers for his proclamation of the word, it was so that his listeners would understand his word as the effective word of the Lord; as something that is not only to be heard but that must become a deed in the listener. That was the purpose of the Incarnation: the Son became one like us so that we could become like he is; that is, persons who understand existence as a mission and make it a reality among those who are followers. Thus Paul can be comforted by brethren who, after receiving the word, correctly pass it on; their fruits show him the fruit of the Lord. He can endure having to sit still, since this activity is entrusted to them, which gives witness to the genuine activity of the Lord.

4:12. *Epaphras, who is one of yourselves, a servant of Christ Jesus, greets you, always remembering you earnestly in his prayers, that you stand mature and fully assured in all the will of God.*

Epaphras shows that, finally, there is yet another kind of prayer: he fights in prayer for the community. His prayer is hard, soldierly work. It is no longer thanksgiving, no longer worship; it is placing oneself at the disposal of the conversation with God, so that what the praying person desires in faith might be attained. The Colossians are the object of this work, that is: through prayer they are to be worked upon, through the prayer of one of their own who, first, is acquainted with them and, second, knows to what place he desires to bring them. In this prayer mountains must be moved; it is an ongoing, laborious struggle that this man has, yet he does not admonish his fellow believers to pray more so that they may become more perfect, but instead he wants to bring this about through his own prayer before God. He stands before God as the representative of the Colossians and demands: that they may *stand mature and fully assured*. They should persevere, not grow weary in the faith, and consequently God should be able to fulfill them more and more, to transform them according to *the will of God*, so that they may become *mature*. They are like a heavy stone that has to be carried away from a hidden place to another, where it will be exposed to the weathering effects of sun, rain and wind. Epaphras does this carrying, but the decisive influence is left to God. And yet it is not left solely to God's judgment, since faith has inspired Epaphras with the conviction that there is nothing better for his neighbors than to do whatever pertains to God's will in the fullness of faith. Earlier, when Paul asked for the prayers of the Colossians, he was actively involved in this prayer. Now Epaphras takes on the entire activity; the Colossians are passive insofar as they did nothing to become the objects of his prayer; but from this passivity arises new activity, because Epaphras, with God's leave, has set to work on them so that God will make them perfect. This process of reworking sooner or later will bring them to join in the disciple's prayer, to participate in the conversation with God and also to add their share of suffering to what Epaphras suffers in the battle. Nothing is mentioned of any special consolation or relief that Epaphras gains by this work; only that he is storming heaven. He is wrestling with God so as to carry out his, the petitioner's, will, and yet the result must be that in doing so he accomplishes God's will.

4:13. *For I bear him witness that he has worked hard for you and for those in Laodicea and in Hierapolis.*

Paul declares here that he has an insight into the laborious prayer of Epaphras. Maybe he has noticed, first of all, how much time he spends at it but probably also the special circumstances of his prayer. It is likely that when he prays he does not just leave it at that but, rather, supports his prayer requests with penance and fasting, things that Paul can observe without difficulty. We can suspect that Epaphras has told him, too, how much he has taken the welfare of the community to heart. And Paul has seen the connection quite clearly: between the faith and prayer of the disciple, between prayer and what accompanies and supports it, between the disciple's efforts and the community. And so he issues a testimonial. One who prays has the power to bring his own nearer to God, so to commend those entrusted to him to eternal life, even during their lifetime, that a displacement occurs, that something of this earthly life shifts into eternity and is taken into divine custody. Those who are affected do not need to know it at the moment; the fruit will be present nonetheless. Earthly life is not only under the influence of eternal life; it actually borrows from it regular patterns of being, which alter it. Perhaps Paul has noticed something of this transformation in the three communities; and since he is acquainted with Epaphras' efforts, he can make the connection between cause and effect. When he conveys this to the Colossians, it is to spur them on to more prayer of their own or to strengthen their faith in the efficacy of prayer and to inspire gratitude for their intercessor. Paul testifies to this fruitfulness by his very office: by his will and his duty to make what is fruitful in Christianity even more fruitful by proclamation.

4:14. *Luke the beloved physician and Demas greet you.*

The two are mentioned together, yet with a difference; they send greetings together, but Luke is distinguished as the *beloved physician*. He is the only one whose occupation Paul notes, probably due to the consideration that Luke's work as a physician is not without significance for the apostolate of Paul's circle. It cannot be otherwise: Luke holds a very special position, through his occupation, through Paul's affection for him; his greeting should be weighed in this connection. He is an apostle, a friend of Paul, and yet he remains a physician by placing his occupation at the service of his apostolate; in this regard Paul's mention of his occupation plays a role similar to that of the local origins of the others who belong to the Colossians. One's circle, one's walk of life, whether it be an occupation or a place of birth, plays a part in the consequences that one's faith will have, in the form that one's mission and apostolate will take—perhaps not directly affecting the plan of God, who calls souls, but certainly in the Church and in human society. A physician comes into contact with other people as any apostle would; he can administer the bodily remedies that his clients seek from him in such a way that they correspond to Christian teachings and attitudes. When Paul at the end of his letter lists various kinds of prayer, it is always in connection with particular persons who pray; there is an anonymous corporate prayer of the Church, but there are also the graphic features of the individual, which can be used to demonstrate a particular aspect of it. Many believers are called to and encouraged in the faith in a very specific way by an acquaintance with particular paths that others have followed, and this may be even more true of particular paths to the apostolate.

4:15. *Give my greetings to the brethren at Laodicea and to Nympha and the church in her house.*

The greetings that Paul conveys are connected with his responsibilities, are mixed in with doctrinal demands and include instructions on prayer. And now he asks the Colossians to pass the greetings on, precisely because it is a matter of apostolic greetings. It is up to them, therefore, to extend them to others, according to the measure of their faith, their readiness and their mission. Paul selects those who are to be greeted: the brethren of another community collectively and then a particular believer and her household. This is like a small church within the Church, a house inside God's house. The household serves as a model, then, for the Church universal. And similarly, the personal greeting is in turn a model for greetings in general; every one of those addressed in the letter can imagine that he, too, has been singled out for a personal greeting, without diminishing what is special in the ones sent to the Laodiceans or to Nympha and her household. The Church consists of ordered members; there are gatherings into groups and communities, and there are scatterings, and between them there are individuals. The things that go on in the Church should be as full of life as possible. This domestic community appears as an image for the compact nature of the Church; it is the bit of leaven in the middle of the dough; other communities are at a distance, and yet the same words and demands apply to them, too, since they belong to the same Church.

4:16. And when this letter has been read among you, have it read also in the church of the Laodiceans; and see that you read also the letter from Laodicea.

Just as the word of God, in order to stay alive, must not only be accepted but also passed on, so too the letter of the Apostle. It should be forwarded to the other community, and vice versa. An exchange is foreseen, with the purpose of enlivening instruction. An exchange that at the same time means succession, a beginning and a continuation. It is an image of the Christian's life in the Church, which brings ongoing changes between times of secular career work, of prayer, and of hearing the word. Or in the case of the priest and the religious: the most varied activities, which all revolve around the word of God, in action as in contemplation, preaching, chanting in choir, spiritual reading, meditation. Each permeates the rest, is the expression of the same thing; in everything the believer fits into a larger church choir. The same "now this, now that" is illustrated by the exchange of letters: now it is the letter that was written for the Colossians personally, especially meant for them and read by them; then again it is the letter to Laodicea, which at first sight seems to have less to do with the Colossians and yet upon reading will show that it is intended precisely for them, too, that it is meaningful and fruitful for them as was their own, that they are led by other trains of thought and circumstances to the same things: to prayer and self-giving and work for the greater glory of God. With this arrangement Paul wants to strengthen the community's sense of catholicity. He wants no sects, no separated fields of endeavor.

Whether spoken to directly or indirectly, all should listen and answer with the same spontaneity.

4:17. *And say to Archippus, "See that you fulfil the ministry which you have received in the Lord."*

A personal admonition. Every office that the Church confers is conferred by the Lord, who does not go away even for a moment from the Church that he founded. In every mission and installation in office he is present and confers the office from and as part of his own mission. Everyone who has an office should stand before the Lord always conscious of this. His office is on loan from the Lord; he must take good care of it. It never loses the character of coming this very minute from the Lord, of always being accompanied by him. But he who holds it must attend to it. It cannot be determined whether Paul's words contain a reproach or not. Certainly it is an admonition intended to strengthen the relation of Archippus to his service. He should become watchful again, just as every believer always has in faith the opportunity of awakening anew. In the gift of the Eucharist the Lord proves his constant and ever undiminished living presence. Every consecrated Host has the same fullness of life. But every office in the Church, too, is a living gift of the living Lord. In Eucharist and office the Church possesses this perpetual liveliness of the Lord, his being here, his working, so that every believer stands before him, prays before him, and before him attends to the duties of his office. And through this presence in faith, this "seeing and not seeing", he gains insight into the entire world of the Lord. The Church is not a self-contained space. The Church is not bound to passing time or to a limited earthly place (in which the Lord might be thought to have shown himself especially alive). The Church is the presence, indeed the living presence of eternity in time, a prospect of heaven from earth's point of view, and this in faith, and believers must subordinate themselves to its efficacy. Faith is not efficacious because a person with some qualification or other exercises certain faculties for the benefit of the Christian faith; faith is efficacy itself, the living presence; already on earth it provides access to the heavenly mysteries in such a way that they with their celestial logic, in their essential being, are not disturbed but can remain what they are. And the place of believing is the Church. She is the place of the eternal, the per-during place, the place of commitment to permanence. Therefore the Church can admonish the Church: *See that you fulfil the ministry.* The one with the most responsibility is the one who holds the office or who confers one, who has to awaken the faith of others and through his word keeps alive the hope of the living Church. The responsibility of the entire Church should not be narrowed down or weakened; it is always whole in the entire Church, just as it has to be whole in the slightest concern of those who take positions of service. A subordinate service is no excuse for second-class, diminished responsibility. Just as the Son, being the second Person of the Blessed Trinity, who comes from the Father and does his will, nevertheless always remains consubstantially God, so too does a person who has a subordinate office in the Church share in the entire responsibility; indeed every believer remains, in the presence of the Church, the Lord and the triune God, a bearer of the whole gift of grace, which he must manage with careful stewardship.

4:18. *I, Paul, write this greeting with my own hand. Remember my fetters. Grace be with you.*

Paul sends greetings as a man and as an apostle, and his signature gives evidence of this twofold concern: of the man and of the pastor. But the greeting that seals and summarizes the entire letter leads to a new admonition: *Remember my fetters.* The conclusion is a new beginning. Now that they have finished with the letter and set eyes on the signature, they should be conscious of the Apostle's situation and, in light of that, think and pray over all they have heard. Pulling everything together in this way is at the same time a symbol for everything that takes place in the Church, for the liturgical year or for the vital sacramental system or for the hierarchical structure; because everything about her is always true in all ways. And the individual thing that is true is so always in combination with everything else that is true in the faith. What is singled out returns to the unity, but what is tied in again with the rest can also, according to the circumstances and need, be taken by any corner, just as prayer can be, and then it is again this individual thing, existing in itself, which still, despite its individuation, encompasses the value of the totality. Just as the office of the individual embodies the universal office, so this final greeting embraces everything that is in the letter; it serves to underline it and simultaneously to impress upon the memory the picture of Paul and his fetters, so that the readers will not have the teaching before their eyes without the person, nor the person without the teaching.

Grace be with you. The grace of the Lord, who founded the Church, the grace of the Lord, who sends his servants to do battle, the grace of the Lord, who confers upon every prayer such a fullness that the person praying experiences anew this grace, which draws and encloses his entire being into the Lord. Every hearer of this last word can interpret it according to the needs of his own prayer life. It is a living word, which points back to the presence of the Lord's life and includes the believers, but which also dispenses everything the Lord holds in readiness for the individual, the Church and the whole redeemed world: grace.